The Devil's Punchbowl

The Devil's Punchbowl

A Cultural and Geographic Map of California Today

Edited by

KATE GALE

&

VERONIQUE DE TURENNE

Red Hen Press | Pasadena, CA

Book layout by Mark E. Cull and Sydney Nichols
Photograph selections by Veronique de Turenne

The devil's punchbowl: a cultural and geographic map of California today / edited by Kate Gale and Veronique de Turenne.—1st ed.
    p. cm.
 ISBN 978-1-59709-164-0
 1. California—Description and travel. 2. California—Social life and customs. 3. California—Geography. 4. California—Biography. I. Gale, Kate. II. De Turenne, Veronique.
 F866.2.D48 2010
 979.4—dc22

                              2010019152

The Annenberg Foundation, the James Irvine Foundation, the Los Angeles County Arts Commission, and the National Endowment for the Arts partially support Red Hen Press.

First Edition

Published by Red Hen Press
Pasadena, CA
www.redhen.org

Acknowledgements

Some of these essays previously appeared in these publications: "Eternity in an Hour" by David Ulin: *LA Weekly*, Vol. 25, No. 27, May 23-29, 2003; "Thirteen Ways of Seeing Nature in L.A." by Jenny Price: *Believer*, April/May 2006 and earlier version in *Land of Sunshine: An Environmental History of Metropolitan Los Angeles*, 2005; "Kaddish for a Coyote" is an excerpt from "The Other Side of Los Angeles" by Deanne Stillman: *LA City Beat*, February 7, 2008; "In the Shadow of the San Gabriels" and "Twenty-four Hours in the Life of a California Oak" by Thomas Curwen: *Los Angeles Times*; "Light: Sunrise and Shadow, Majesty and Menace—How Very L.A." by David St. John: *Los Angeles Magazine*; "The Pictures-Perfect City," "Our True Heartthrob," and "Land of Reinvention" by Patt Morrison: *Los Angeles Times*.

Los Angeles Public Library: "Boarding the Red Car Special." Copyright © 1948, courtesy of the Los Angeles Public Library.

Stuart Molder: "Tufas and High Clouds—Mono Lake bw." May 3, 2005 via Flickr, Creative Commons Attribution.

Robert Garcia: "Woman's Building." July 16, 2007 via Flickr, Creative Commons Attribution.

Celeste Freeman: "110 Freeway at 105 Freeway." October 1, 2008 via Flickr, Creative Commons Attribution

Kimberly Perkins: "Carrizo Plain—Western Rattlesnake." Copyright © 2008 by Kimberly Perkins. All rights reserved.

Harold Morby: "Dodger Stadium." Copyright © 1962, courtesy of the Los Angeles Public Library.

Los Angeles Public Library: "Panoramic View, Chavez Ravine." Courtesy of the Los Angeles Public Library.

Julio J. Bermejo: "Valley Blvd. Sign." Copyright © 2008 by Julio J. Bermejo.

M. Kasahara: "This Receipt Is Wonderful . . ." February 3, 2009 via Flickr, Creative Commons Attribution.

Ernest Marquez: "32 Foot Long Shark." Copyright © by Ernest Marquez.

Los Angeles Public Library: "View of Plaza Church." Courtesy of the Los Angeles Public Library.

Raymond Shobe: "Coyote in the Road, Kelso, California 09.15.2007." September 15, 2007 via Flickr, Creative Commons Attribution.

Thomas Hawk: "Circus Liquor." December 27, 2008 via Flickr, Creative Commons Attribution.

Mark Coggins: "Johnny Mercer." December 31, 2008 via Flickr, Creative Commons Attribution.

Smithsonian Institution: "Yurok Canoe on the Trinity River." Courtesy of the Smithsonian Institution.

army.arch: "Los Angeles, CA Central Library 1971." August 9, 2008 via Flickr, Creative Commons Attribution.

George "toastforbrekkie": "Ignition." April 2, 2008 via Flickr, Creative Commons Attribution.

Glenn Hightree: "Anza-Borrego Desert." April 1, 2008 via Flickr, Creative Commons Attribution.

Los Angeles Public Library: "Headstone for Woman." Courtesy of the Los Angeles Public Library.

Los Angeles Public Library: "Chinese railroad workers near Lang." Courtesy of the Los Angeles Public Library.

David St. John: "Rock Light." November 20, 2005 via Flickr, Creative Commons Attribution.

Ernest Marquez: "Women Dancing on Rock." Copyright © by Ernest Marquez.

revertebrate: "Star Anise." March 21, 2008 via Flickr, Creative Commons Attribution.

Marc Lambrechts: "Coriander Flowers." June 17, 2007 via Flickr, Creative Commons Attribution.

Nick "niznoz": "Pepper." March 27, 2007 via Flickr, Creative Commons Attribution.

Joshua Wickerham: "Tuomg Duc Me Khoc." December 18, 2005 via Flickr, Creative Commons Attribution.

Karen "unsure shot": "That Way to Safety." April 12, 2006 via Flickr, Creative Commons Attribution.

Contents

for Steve Wasserman

The Devil's Punchbowl

We wanted to write a living history of California, to collect pieces by living authors who breathed in California and loved it, who loved the desert, the mountains, the beaches, the freeways, the smog. We found them. Carolyn See writing about the coming of the smog; writers on Mono Lake, the Devil's Punchbowl, Arcata, the restaurant where the most drug deals go down in California. The best river for fishing. Mark Arax writes of Tulare Lake, a buried lake like Atlantis that resurfaced and California is all about reinvention no matter who does the reinventing. Susan Straight writes of the Inland Empire a place that is maybe past reinvention. She talks of immigrants, of working hard of raising children in spite of difficulties in desert heat. Jenny Factor writes of the oldest Jewish cemetery. California is full of stories. "Kettleman City" by Matt Shears is one of those pieces that surprises you; it's a city we've all driven through on our way to San Francisco but have never really seen, and that apparently is the problem. The city houses a chemical waste dump, a 70% Latino population, 25% unemployment and an insanely high cancer rate and birth defect rate. That's California too. As Pat Morrison says of the car, the symbol of California, "it runs on fossil fuel and faith and myth."

This is a book about California with its dreams of sunshine, gold, light, oranges, fruit trees, palms, pools, silicon and then the reality: Mountains and brush, miles of coastline, smog and redwoods, deserts and Joshua Trees, drugs and poverty, sadness and something we hold in our hands instead of sunlight, instead of money, instead of dreams. "String or nothing" the hobbit might say. That's it, in California, what you have is not what you expected, but what you have you make the best of and you create a new story with that, you create a story that will make your geographic space the envy of the world. That's California. Don't you wish you were here? Don't you wish you were a Californian too?

"Boarding the Red Car Special"

Carolyn See

The people in the house behind us had a dovecote. Early every morning I woke to a fusillade of cooing, and looked out my window at a feathery palm tree where another flock of birds set up a racket. The window would be open and the scent of roses filled the room year round: my parents' house—a small yellow Craftsman on a tidy street filled with other houses like it—boasted a hundred foot bank of Cecile Brunner roses that continuously bloomed. The roses were mixed in with honeysuckle. It was before the end of World War II and the air was sparkling clean. Cars were still scarce. Except for when it rained, the sky maintained a piercing blue, the trimmed lawns stayed as green as they could be. It looked like Paradise to me, our little world in Eagle Rock. So safe we never thought about it being safe. Little girls could walk twelve blocks along Colorado Boulevard to Saint Dominic's Elementary without a hint of fear.

Gas was rationed. Ubiquitous signs asked, "Is this trip really necessary?" My mother walked a block to the corner grocery. She was beautiful, and a besotted butcher saved the best cuts of meat for her, whether she had the ration stamps for them or not. Our way to the outside world (downtown Los Angeles) was the street-car, the No. 5 Yellow Car, which came to the end of the line at the corner of Colorado and Townsend Avenue, where we lived. The rails just stopped there, at our street, proving once again our lives were blessed.

My father took the No. 5 car to work every morning, to save gas. One day he got on while the conductor was still taking a break. The guy had his nose buried in a pulp magazine. Daddy saw he was reading one of his own stories, maybe the first or second he had ever sold. He waited until the conductor had finished, then asked, as casually as he could manage, "How'd you like the story?" The conductor answered, "It's good, but it got pretty rough when some ranch hand poured whiskey in a cowboy's eyes." Pretty rough! My dad never forgot that morning. He himself was a soft-spoken advertising man with a store of silly jokes and goofy behavior. Pretty rough!

Just before the streetcar started, the conductor would swing through it, flipping chair backs from one side of the slatted wooden seats to the other. There were handles on each chair back, and he used a deft, forward, nonchalant motion, changing them all in one long clatter. Then he'd move from what had just been the back of the car to what was now the front. There were three sections to each car; the middle part had windows to close against the weather, the sections on either end were open to the air.

On December 8th, the Feast of the Immaculate Conception and a holiday at Saint Dominic's, my mother would take me on the streetcar downtown to go Christmas shopping. She wore heels and hose, a good suit and a nice hat. Everybody dressed up when they went downtown. We always stopped at Bullock's, which in those days had performed a tremendous courtesy for little kids; they'd built an immense, gently sloping, smooth and slick wooden slide which descended from one whole floor to another. Our mothers shopped; we slid and slid, never tired of it.

Children didn't need their parents to make the trip downtown. By the time we were eight or nine, we were allowed to go to the movies in groups of three. Good Catholic mothers entrusted their daughters to the larger world without a second thought. Our only fear was that we might absent-mindedly take the wrong car home, but we never did. We looked for the yellow car with the big 5 on it, and we were fine.

Other times, my dad would go off on a hunting weekend. My mother would put on her good suit and a hat with a little veil. She'd click down Townsend Avenue in her high heels, and we'd be off to the races, as she liked to say. We'd see the Ballet Russe de Monte Carlo if it was in town, but what mother really liked was going over to the Million Dollar Theatre, where you could find more raffish entertainment. We saw Nellie Lutched, who sang, "Fetch it on down to my house, daddy! Ain't nobody home but me!" or, "They have a drink called pousse cafe, you drink it from a cup. You do not feel it going down, but man, when it comes up!" We came home from that particular afternoon, and my mother spent the long summer evening trying to float Grand Marnier on top of Crème de Cacao and brandy on top of that, with little success but lots of perseverance.

Another time we went to see Josephine Baker, who spent a couple of hours walking back and forth on the stage of the Million Dollar with very little clothes and a series of great big headdresses. I was only nine years old; I didn't get the point, but mother explained to me on the streetcar home that Baker had come all the way from

Paris to Los Angeles to do these shows and that actually, in Paris, she was apt not to wear anything at all.

Looking back on this now, I wonder where we got the money, and what my mother was thinking. She and my dad, who'd worked for the cool *Los Angeles Daily News* in the old days before he'd gotten his job as an advertising man, would throw poker parties for a bunch of disreputable journalists, including Matt Weinstock, whose columns had been collected in a book called *Muscatel at Noon*. My parents had some boisterous times together, but they never seemed to go out on an actual date. Most weekends he'd be gone, hunting, so it would be my mother who took us back, again, to the Million Dollar, where, between sets of mariachi music, we'd see one of the widows of Pancho Villa, who came out on stage and took a bow, to tumultuous applause. Then there was a wait, in the dusk, for the streetcar, the ride to the end of the line, the walk home. The doves would have started their clamor, and my mother, composed and seemingly serene, would make us tomato soup, or creamed tuna on toast. Then bed. If my dad hadn't come home by then, I could sometimes get in with her and listen to the races from Santa Anita or Hollywood Park being called by Joe Hernandez.

He hadn't really gone hunting, or course. He was out with dozens of girlfriends. He had his own plan, I saw later. He would establish himself as a writer again, starting with pulp magazines and advancing to the slicks. Then he would leave his wife. After he sold his sixth story to the pulps, he did just that. We'd moved from pretty Eagle Rock to an amorphous place on the Micheltorena Hill where there wasn't any neighborhood. Daddy took the books and the records and the pictures and left the house and me to my mother. The woman I had thought of as my mother disappeared forever. Her crazy behavior made her loathed by all her family. My dad got off scot-free, charming at all times, as he went through a passel of women, and two more wives.

My mother made sponge cake with chocolate buttercream frosting, in the old days. She planted nasturtiums and watered the lawn wearing shorts, with a cigarette dangling from her curved lips. During the war we ate steak, because of her. She tended that bank of Cecile Brunner roses.

Then the smog came.

"Tufas and High Clouds"

Charles Hood

From outer space it looks like a road-killed blue donut, roughly ten miles by ten, with a black volcano in the middle covered by the dirty confetti of 80,000 connubial seagulls. Mono Lake exists on the high, Tibetan steppe of a sagebrush desert and, from Highway 395, it looks like a pond on the moon, all the more so as you swing down closer and start to pass the first stucco spires of tufa, a cross between movie-prop stalagmites and termite mounds. Park and walk the boardwalk and dip a finger, tasting: Mono Lake looks like water yet is slimy and bitter and surprisingly frigid. In the 1950s, it was a stand-in for Krakatoa in a bad history movie. Later, Clint Eastwood's *High Plains Drifter* was shot here, as was the cover for Pink Floyd's *Wish You Were Here*. Scanning out today from the crusty, bathtub-ring shoreline, one might see five hundred wild swans or a million and a half eared grebes—or maybe just a killdeer or two and miles of empty saltiness. It depends on the month and the state of the bloom of four trillion sea monkeys.

Go ahead, kids, try this at home. The recipe comes from the Mono Lake Committee's website but is widely agreed to be accurate. To make Mono Lake in your kitchen, start with a big pot. Add a gallon of snowmelt. Heat. Now add eighteen tablespoons of baking soda, ten tablespoons of table salt, eight tablespoons of Epsom salt, a handful of Borax or the most caustic laundry soap you can find, and a pinch or two of strontium, magnesium, arsenic, lithium, iodine, tungsten, and plutonium. Repeat as necessary until you have enough water to cover Santa Monica sixty feet deep.

Mark Twain was here in 1862 and wrote about it in *Roughing It*. He had more fun having a bad time than anybody since Virgil in the *Georgics* described all the ways a sheep can get sick and die (and there are a lot). According to Wikipedia, Cinderella shot a video here, though they are not my band so I report that as hearsay. If the visual cliché of the 2008 elections was a Prius at Trader Joe's with an Obama bumper sticker, in the '80s it would have been a beater truck with "Save Mono Lake" on one of its sagging bumpers. Starting in 1941, L.A.'s Department of Water and Power began drinking up all of the input creeks, which in turn (via evaporation) concentrated salts and so on, turning Mono Lake into a toxic sump. This is bad, because a native kind of shrimp and a scuba-diving fly are an essential part of migration's Big Picture. No shrimp, then no birds, simple math. Meanwhile, falling lake levels meant that the islands the snowy plovers and California gulls nested on were linked by spits to the mainland, and oh boy, the coyotes were loving it. Cue up the bumper stickers: lawsuits were started, rallies held, T-shirts sold. In the end Los Angeles had to agree to put some of the water back, maintaining a sustainable lake and moderately intact riparian corridors spidering down from Yosemite like small green gardens. The 1994 court decision secretly shocked many eco-warriors. Us'n plain folks—the little guys—won one against The Man. Right on.

Shrimp drive everything at Mono Lake, or, rather, what four or five or six trillion brine shrimp don't feed in the main lake, the edge of flies slathered along the summer shore make up for in equal balance. Even the Native Americans called themselves Fly Eaters. They harvested the pupae of Mono Lake's alkali flies in mail bag-sized reed baskets held in place by tump lines, and when the harvest was dried in the sun and hulled, it looked like mounds of yellow rice. At fifteen calories per rice grain and with an ideal balance of fat and protein, the dried fly pupae sustained indigenous populations up and down the Eastern Sierra and across into Yosemite Valley. Today, the alkali flies feed resident and migrant birds—phalaropes and gulls and avocets and Brewer's blackbirds—and as bugs go, are among the noblest flies invented since they do not bite and are indifferent to people and, in fact, scurry out of the way if you walk along the shore in late summer and take pictures of the tufa towers and smile at how the swallows loop and bank, Peaceable Kingdom from cumulous to cow patties.

The title of a very good painting by Albert Bierstadt would have been *Mono Lake by Moonlight.* Not to praise aesthetics beyond all reason, but under a full moon in winter, the place has to be the most beautiful toxic sump in America. It is worth going just for that. The whole Eastern Sierra is often heart-breakingly beautiful, especially in winter, when the mountains themselves are more snowy and sheer than any normal god would allow. Dominant plant is sagebrush, genus *Artemisia,* the name of a small press and also the center of a poem by Gary Snyder, "Earrings Dangling and Miles of Desert," in *Mountains and Rivers Without End.* In my copy of *Native American Ethnobotany,* the entries for things to do with all the varieties of Artemisia run for eleven single-spaced pages; let's just say that if everything outside of the city limits looks like a drab grey bush to you, you have 20,000 years of catching up to do.

The history of incest is the history of history because otherwise, how can we explain such screwball, inbred, goiter-necked facts as a Mono Lake, post-Indian and pre-Tioga Pass last-chance gas station, which had its own railroad (to ferry vanilla-scented old-growth Jeffrey Pine to the mines of Bodie and Aurora), its own steamers (ditto, plus ore, coming back), its own fish food factory (still extant, beneath a hill north of Lee Vining), its own pumice mine (also still extant, and you pass it and the county dump and a few very recent cinder cones on the way to the South Tufa parking lot), and its own rutabaga farm? The history of the Indians killing the Indians and then the whites killing the Indians that the Indians didn't kill is nauseatingly archetypal, so we can skip over that, but I suppose we should linger on Cold War images of the U.S. Navy detonating massive underwater explosions to film the tsunamis coming ashore, just to figure out what an atom bomb does, exactly. The barracks are gone but there is an S.S. Minnow white propeller and a bronze plaque on the dirt road that leads down to the place where you put in kayaks, still called today Navy Beach. One wants it to make sense, yet somehow visit after visit, it never quite does. Cf. Anne Carson: "Anthropology is a science of mutual surprise."

Anne Carson said too, "We live by waters breaking out of the heart." This comes from *Plainwater*, via "The Anthropology of Water." She was talking about me, about a time when I was a new stepdad and I took the kids to Mono Lake. We stayed in a motel and went hiking and found the weathered hull of a plank boat overturned in the brush. In the pictures the boys are wearing my Patagonia gloves, which is odd because they kept losing them, two or three pair a day, so as I recall, by that day of the trip everybody was out of gloves, and also hats, extra sweaters, and clean underwear. I was in love with their mother the way a volcano loves the sky and so is always surprised when the great photogenic arcs of magma suddenly hit the glass ceiling of gravity and splash back down defeated on the sides of the fissure. I mean this not as sexual reference but in the sense that hardening into asphalt is a surprise for anybody.

Geography is memory in three ways. One is that you will always be disappointed with Paris or the Sahara since to go at all to a place, not only do they speak French, but first you learned about it from National Geographic television specials or a chapter in school, so the reality will never be as good as cinematography's promises. Two is that after you go, you can replay the scenes and make them better. Even if you hated it, your hatred perfects itself. Three is that places make no sense if we are honest and listen to the broken water of our hearts. Instead of objective geography,

CHARLES
HOOD

place means the place where you got a speeding ticket or heard a kind of bird that sounded like bent wire or first learned that if you kiss with your tongue you probably should first wear rubber-soled shoes and other non-conductive clothing. I am sorry that Mono Lake is now a National Scenic Postcard Area, sorry that people now know, because it was just mine first—a discarded, dirt-road kind of place to sleep in my truck on climbing trips, waking up in a North Face down bag facing the tufa domes where the South Parking Lot is now (no camping allowed, $3 per person entrance fee), a place that glowed numinously as the sun came up and I peed in the sagebrush and everything in my body, my world, my horizon was alive with possibility. Later this place became something more necessary and even more holy, a pilgrimage site (and still an illegal camping stop) as I made the Hank Williams drive from L.A. to Bridgeport or Reno on visitation weekends to pick up my daughter whose mom, like an errant comet, lived her life in parabolas. I needed the centering it gave me, not so much beauty as the certainty that I could do this, it would be all right, I could keep my temper and write the checks and make the drives and above all find the small happy place in the world for my daughter and me to exist as a family. An odd family, to be sure, as odd as the towers of South Tufa made out of spackle and toothpaste, but a family, dammit, now and forever. There is something about the way some kinds of light come to you that is indelible and sustaining, not as in an abstract word like faith but as a hard, real thing, light that pushes you back on your feet or goes into your eyes through your ribs. There are some very good, artistically satisfying photographs of Mono Lake (Galen Rowell, et al.) but as with photographs of Notre Dame or the Sahara, they are Other to the reality of what you will remember yourself if you go to Mono Lake or maybe if you have been or if the State of California says you may see your children on alternate Saturdays and once extra at Christmas. Our bodies inhabit reality not in the present but in the fog and brushfire of expectation and memory, so that Mono Lake can mean a bumper sticker and Mark Twain even as it also can mean that the ducks look like trash out past that little island and that once, in East Africa, a British guide was fast-forwarding through bird tapes he had recorded in America, and he happened to stop on a sweet, churring *wheeurr,* which is the song of a Sage Thrasher, and it takes you directly back to a time when you slept in your truck one March morning at Mono Lake, and how when you woke up a Sage Thrasher was teed-up on the eldest, most six-foot-tall sage, singing a song just like that, and there you were, in Africa yet about to cry you were smiling so hard with happiness and the burning incandescence of memory.

Dana Goodyear

Late in summer, when the Van Duzen, a tributary of the Eel, begins to clot with rich, bright-green algae, the children of Bridgeville, California, get the river itch and stop going in the water. Instead, the kids, with names like Sonrize and Nervona and Crystal ride dirt bikes down the town's one street, which is lined with Himalaya berries, wild fennel, and falling-down kit-houses painted pastel colors. They wander back and forth across the old stone bridge, built in 1925 and closed to traffic several years ago, or drift into the post office for a piece of free candy. One hopeful day each August, the townspeople hold a festival, and everyone dresses up in alien costumes. There is a competition to see whose homemade UFO can fly the farthest when launched from the old bridge. The grown-ups try earnestly to win. They know best how hard it is to get away.

Bridgeville is in Humboldt County, geographically and psychologically sited, locals say, "behind the Redwood Curtain"—meaning that as a place and frame of mind it is as incongruous with outside reality as the world past the furs in C.S. Lewis's attic wardrobe. It is an out-of-the-way place, with thirty or so residents, and not a single restaurant, bar, or business of any sort. But the town itself is a kind of enterprise: it is privately owned. It became famous in 2002 when its owners, a family called Lapple, offered it for sale on eBay, with a $775,000 minimum.

The Lapples had bought the place in 1973, for $150,000. Four years later, the Pentecostal Faith Challengers, a congregation from Fremont, bought it for $450,000 after their preacher heard an advertisement for it on the radio. The parishioners sold their homes to raise cash for a down payment, with the Lapples financing the rest of the deal. When the Challengers arrived, they found, according to *Time* magazine, "a rural slum in the middle of God's country"—trashed cars, broken septic tanks, buildings in disrepair. They renovated the café and banned alcohol and tobacco from the general store, where they held their first service, singing a hymn to the tune of "Okie from Muskogee": "I'm proud to be a Christian in Bridgeville / A place where repentant sinners can have a ball / We don't smoke marijuana in Bridgeville / As a matter of fact, we don't smoke at all." Prayer services rang through the valley, spooking the ranchers. "We came up over the ridge and my husband's mule, Gomer, looked down there like, What is this?" the matriarch of an old ranching family told me. "They'd put up speakers. We said we should put up a speaker on our mountain and say, 'Amen.' It's not that we're not religious, but . . ." Before too long, the preacher disappeared, his congregation followed, and Bridgeville belonged once more to the Lapples.

When the Lapples put Bridgeville on eBay, they advertised it as "a private retreat, basking in the glory of the redwoods" and a possible "economic powerhouse with the potential for generating a large cash flow." The prospect of owning a zip code was compelling and novel. Ideas for Bridgeville ranged from corporate getaway to hairdressers' camp and stuntman training ground. At the frothiest moment of the eBay bidding war, which rose to $1.8 million before falling through, one contender suggested turning it into a brothel. Eventually, an Orange County mortgage banker bought the town, for $700,000, thinking he'd make it over into a mind-body health resort modeled on Esalen. He sold it—nearly doubling his money, in 2006—when he realized that he and his wife and children were quite happy in Laguna Hills, and he didn't want to end up like the Harrison Ford character in *Mosquito Coast*.

People in Bridgeville remember the FBI coming in moon suits in 1999 when someone reported seeing a vial marked "Anthrax Bio-Hazard-Culture" in a Quonset hut at the edge of town; they remember the body of a "cooker" found out on the highway; they talk about big meth labs run by the Mexican Mafia, and they know who's growing what and where and that you're not allowed to wonder aloud how anyone makes his money. But the worst crime anyone in Bridgeville can remember is the murder of Joey Church. It was in 2003, when word about the little bit of Humboldt county paradise for sale had been circulating on the Internet. One day that May, a Paso Robles man named Thomas Applegate picked up two friends who were whiling away the morning at a casino, did some speed, drove up to Bridgeville, and took a look around. "When we pulled into the little town, he says, 'This is what I want to buy,'" one of his friends testified later. "''Cause I even heard it's for sale on the Internet, awhile back.'" Then, according to this friend, "He just drove through nice and slow and said, 'Well, we'll put your mom over here, we're going to be over here,'" and so on like that, passing the little pastel houses, including the one where

Joey Church, a sweet-tempered man, legally blind, was playing video games with his girlfriend and three kids. Applegate left his friends off at a gas station and drove back to Bridgeville, knocked on Church's door, and said he wanted to buy the house. From the couch, where he was by now watching the season finale of "The Simpsons," Church told him he couldn't buy just the house, he had to buy the whole town, so Applegate shot him dead with a .44-Magnum Colt Anaconda. He was sentenced to seventy-two years to life, but that has not really laid the matter to rest. At the trial, Church's sister said she'd never feel safe in Bridgeville again. It is fair to say that Joey Church's murder crystallized the anxieties people in Bridgeville feel about living in a town that keeps being put up for sale.

Of all those who have projected their fantasies on Bridgeville, the intentions of Danny La Paille, who bought the town in 2006, were probably the purest, and the most misguided. He dreamed of creating a home for his fractured, hard-luck family, far from the stress and crime and pollution of Riverside County, where they lived. His father was ill, and his brother was a petty criminal; he hoped his mother and grandmother, a part-time bookkeeper and the janitorial manager of the Palm Springs School District, who scraped to contribute to the $1.25 million dollar purchase price, would retire there. When he came up from Riverside, he hosted barbeques and talked about civic spirit. He told the residents—his tenants—that he was going to build an eco-friendly store, and create a community center and a playground for the kids.

Everybody loved La Paille. He was handsome and friendly and seemed rich. He was only twenty-five, but drove a new Mercedes roadster and talked about an apparently fictional career as a music manager. Danny La Paille was going to be Bridgeville's salvation: he would get his friend Al Gore to come; his friend Whoopi Goldberg would do a reading at the school. The people of Bridgeville took it hard when, six months after La Paille bought the town, he shot himself through the chest. An anonymous commentator, posting on the Web site of the Eureka *Times Standard*, speculated "maybe the guy shot himself after he realized what a stupid purchase he made."

Not long ago, I heard that Bridgeville had a new buyer. The sellers—La Paille's family—were in escrow with an organization called Nabahood Community Development, which is hoping to buy the town for $1.3 million, and plans to turn the town into a rehabilitation facility for the homeless. Now it's just waiting for stimulus money from the government to help close the deal.

Pam Waterman

Pasadena Gardens

It's an eleven-mile drive from La Cañada's oak-studded Descanso Gardens with its wonderful collection of camellias to San Marino's Huntington Library and Botanical Garden with 14,000 different plant species and cultivars in many different themed gardens. On the journey between these two garden showplaces, you pass several outstanding public gardens that give you a sense of the long history of Pasadena's love affair with gardens.

The garden at the Norton Simon Museum, located on a dramatic piece of land near the Arroyo Seco at the western edge of Pasadena, contains dozens of masterpieces of modern sculpture in a setting that attempts to recreate a feeling for Claude Monet's garden at Giverny. One of Pasadena's famous early gardens, the thirty-two-acre Carmelita, was a local botanical wonder at this location in the 1890s. Now the shimmering pond outside the museum is surrounded by statuary placed on large granite blocks that designer Nancy Goslee Power found in a Fresno quarry where they had languished since 1929.

One block south on Orange Grove Boulevard is the thirty-five-acre former campus of Ambassador College, now the site of Maranatha High School. The campus was assembled in the 1950s and '60s with purchases of older homes and gardens on Orange Grove—once known as "Millionaire's Row." It remains a virtual open-air museum of plants, gardens, and home styles created for the elite who wintered in Pasadena at the turn of the last century. A stroll through the gardens becomes a vivid reminder of the elaborate, lush landscapes they favored for their winter retreats.

On the crest of a steep hill overlooking the nearby Arroyo Seco is an elegant building, once a luxury resort hotel for winter visitors to Pasadena. Now used as the U.S. Ninth Circuit Court of Appeals, the old Vista Del Arroyo Hotel has a long entrance pergola festooned with red and white climbing roses. It is surrounded by lovely plantings, flowering shrubs, a succulent garden and exotic trees. The grounds are a reminder, along with the restored gardens of Ambassador College, of the graceful days when Pasadena was a destination for wealthy Easterners seeking winter sunshine.

A short drive south into the Arroyo Seco takes you to La Casita del Arroyo, a small meeting house and garden built by workmen in the 1930s under the sponsorship of the Pasadena Garden Club. The garden was revitalized in the 1990s by Isabelle Greene, granddaughter of Charles Greene of the team of Greene and Greene, architects of the arts and crafts movement of the early 1900s. The garden is a small jewel of low-maintenance, water-wise landscaping and beautiful views.

A slow drive down Orange Grove Boulevard will convince viewers that cars should be banned from street parking for aesthetic reasons. No automobiles block your view of a graceful planted rhythm of palm trees and magnolias. Although most of the older mansions have been replaced by condominiums, the setbacks are such that the boulevard has a wonderful open feeling and park-like setting. It is one of the most beautiful street scenes in the United States.

A turn east on Arlington Drive takes the viewer to a new garden for Pasadena. On land wrested from Caltrans, a group of citizens have created a Mediterranean-style garden on three acres of land which had been set aside for the completion of the 710 freeway. Lawsuits stalled construction of the freeway and it appears that it will not be built in the form envisioned by Caltrans. Neighbors had had enough of looking at bare land behind their homes and took the initiative in 2005 to create a public garden space on the weed-filled lot. The basic aim of Arlington Garden is to showcase how beautiful and enjoyable a climate-appropriate garden can be.

In the heart of downtown Pasadena is a small treasure of a garden within the heart of the Pacific Asia Museum. Until recently, it was only one of three Chinese gardens in the United States. Grace Nicholson, a collector and dealer of American Indian and Asian art, built herself a Chinese-style home and shop in 1924. When she was carried on a stretcher to the hospital, knowing that it might be her final journey, she asked the men to turn her around so she could have one last look at her beloved *Ginkgo biloba* tree in the patio. The interior Chinese courtyard garden, complete with zigzag bridge and limestone rocks, was designed in 1979.

El Molino Viejo, the old mill, and its garden are located a few blocks south of Pasadena's city limits. As the area's oldest building, dating from the early 1800s, the Old Mill served as a gristmill for nearby Mission San Gabriel, as a golf course clubhouse, a private residence, and now as the headquarters of the Old Mill Foundation.

Though the garden surrounding the Old Mill dates from modern times, it feels very much like the gardens of Early California. Many of the plants are edible, many more natives, and almost all are drought-tolerant. A visit to the Old Mill provides an interesting contrast between the manicured landscapes of nearby homes and the semi-natural grounds of a water-wise, sustainable landscape with a quiet beauty.

The Huntington Library and Botanical Garden also lies just south of Pasadena in adjoining San Marino. A treasure-house of books, art, and plants, the Huntington boasts one of the greatest plant collections in the United States. Every day of the year, plants are blooming and trees are flowering on the 150-acre property. The 101-year-old desert garden is the most famous of the fifteen specialty gardens, but visitors should also see the Japanese Garden, the Rose Garden, the Children's Garden, and the newly completed Chinese garden. The Huntington also has an outstanding collection of camellias, palms, and tropical plants.

"Woman's Building"

Terry Wolverton

STRATIGRAPHY

Some believe there's an electromagnetic grid beneath Earth's surface, unseen by those who walk above. The intersections of this grid are thought to govern placement of sacred sites like the pyramids, to direct the currents of oceans, and even to guide the migration patterns of birds. Skeptics dismiss this as mysticism, not science. Yet one can't deny that some locations seem to summon people to converge there, seem to inspire action, fecundity, and production over decades or centuries.

There's a stretch of land in downtown Los Angeles—bounded by Chinatown and the L.A. River, the base of the Elysian Hills and Lincoln Heights—that has, over centuries, known many extraordinary uses. Those who occupied it rarely knew of its earlier incarnations. In my first decades in Los Angeles I knew it as a railroad yard, stretched out beside the building re-purposed to nourish the vision of a feminist future. I had no thought for who or what was there before the trains. In the 1990s, the rail yard was sold, its tracks unstitched from the earth; I saw the land abandoned, neglected. In 2003, after a decade-long fight by community activists to save it from commercial development, the land was purchased by the state of California and designated a state park.

⁂

State bureaucracies moves slowly and resources are always in short supply. The land looked nothing like a park. Artist Lauren Bon approached the state with a proposal: with funds from the Annenberg Foundation, she would create a massive, temporary, environmental sculpture on the site. This would ease the transition from toxic brownscape to parkland.

19

The site had once been known as the "Cornfield," a nickname believed to have come from the corn that sprouted whenever seed spilled out of the railroad cars. Bon and her team oversaw the effort to clean the land by removing accumulated trash, industrial waste and chemical contaminants. She brought in fifteen hundred truckloads of soil and planted one million seeds of corn. In a nod to Rene Magritte, she titled the artwork, "Not a Cornfield."

⁘

It was certainly not a cornfield during the thirteen years I spent at the Woman's Building, a three-story red brick structure located at the southern end of the North Spring Street Bridge. The Woman's Building housed a feminist art school, galleries, performance space, bookstore, café, thrift store, and offices for several woman-owned businesses and other organizations. The train yard was our backyard. Women came from across the city and around the country to build a different kind of culture, one in which a woman might re-imagine herself and her possibilities.

This was a paradoxical location for such enterprise: Streets of crumbling warehouses next to the tracks. Hobos would leap from boxcars and find temporary refuge under the North Spring Street Bridge, a space we sometimes also commandeered for our performances. Some women were frightened by the shabby men who rode the rails, but they, like we, were only trying to find a way to live more authentically.

Our quest to reinvent the world was fervent. Women had been conquered, rendered invisible; the result was a culture in which the drive for possession and domination had all but annihilated values of cooperation with and respect for living beings and the planet. Western societies had lost their connection to the cycles of sun and moon. In our art making at the Woman's Building, we envisioned a culture transformed. We worked to sing our way into a new world.

The Woman's Building was tucked in a forgotten corner of L.A., but the rent was affordable, and the 18,000 square feet was sufficient to accommodate our activities. To arrive there, one might pass the spires of downtown commerce; the tourist shops of Olvera Street on the site of the original pueblo; the fading, exotic charm of Chinatown.

⁘

Los Angeles' original Chinatown was created by Chinese immigrant laborers who, in the mid-1800s, did the back-breaking work of building the railroad. They established their living quarters just south of the rail yard in which they toiled, land soon to be dubbed The Cornfield.

The River Station opened in 1875 and served as the city's first transcontinental depot and freight yard. For over sixty years, it was the endpoint for restless seekers traveling west toward some imagined future. In its heyday, tracks crisscrossed this land like scars. At one time, 90,000 freight cars were loaded and unloaded at the rail yard each month.

In the late 19th and early 20th century, oil was the region's most important export, and much of it was shipped east by rail. In 1921, the Standard Oil Company built a three-story red brick building on the northeastern tip of the River Yard to house their offices. More than fifty years later, this structure would become the Woman's Building.

∽

Before construction of the rail yard, this land was the site of the primary source of irrigation for the farmlands surrounding *El Pueblo de Nuestra Señora, la Reina de los Angeles* (the Town of Our Lady, the Queen of the Angels), the settlement established in 1781 by mestizos and mulattos under the flag of Spain. The *zanja madre*, or "mother ditch" was an open, earthen trench that ran along the elevated slope at the base of the Elysian Hills. It was fed by a dam of earth and brush, called a *toma*, constructed to divert the river the Spanish called *Porciuncula*. The *zanja madre* carried the water down to the lower elevation of the pueblo; from there it split into multiple ditches channeled to provide for the agricultural needs of the Spanish military.

Spanish rule gave way to Mexican rule gave way to possession of these lands by the United States. Floods washed away the *toma* several times until a wooden one was built. This was subsequently lined with brick.

A vast network of subsidiary channels was developed as the boundaries of the city grew. The *zanja* system was the city's primary source of domestic and irrigation water until 1904. But the persistence of water—the L.A. River was forever flooding—and the seemingly unstoppable expansion of the city necessitated new developments in water systems, and eventually closed the *zanja madre*.

∽

Before the Spanish arrived in 1769, the Tongva Indians had for millennia dwelled in a settlement on the banks of the river, which they called *otcho'o*. Consisting of perhaps 500 huts, this moveable village, which could be relocated as the river flooded or dried, was called *Yangna*.

The Tongva marked time by the swelling and thinning of the moon, called *moar*, but also by the journey of the sun, *tamit*, as it traveled from its northernmost point to its southernmost throughout the year. Summer was considered to have begun when the frogs were heard to croak. During the season of flowers, both women and children adorned themselves with blossoms.

In 1781, the Tongva were forcibly relocated to the San Gabriel Mission, about ten miles from their former settlement, and enslaved. Identifying the natives with the mission, the Spanish would come to call them Gabrielinos.

By the time Anglo historians began to study the Tongva in the mid-1800s, much of the Tongva culture and people had already been decimated by successive waves of invaders. A small, incomplete lexicon of the Tongva language was compiled in the 1850s by Hugo Reid, a white man married to a Tongva wife. One of his observations was that while the Tongva language had many expressions of high regard and affection, it contained no word equivalent to the English word for love. One scholar has observed that the closest correlate is the word, *uisminoc*, which means to sing.

∽

Those of us creating a female future in the 1970s and '80s had no knowledge of the history that lay beneath our feet. Even the river, not one hundred yards east of our front door, was barely known to us. It had been walled off, made invisible. We might drive over the North Spring Street Bridge several times a day without any awareness we were traversing a body of water.

Four decades earlier, between 1934 and 1938, flooding of the always unpredictable river killed 85 people and cost $23 million in damages. In 1938, the Army Corps of Engineers began a twenty-one-year project, completed in 1959, to encase the river in concrete, converting it from a natural waterway to a flood control channel. When I arrived in Los Angeles in 1976, the concrete banks of the river were littered with trash; its waters were reduced to a trickle and polluted by storm run-off, its wildlife nearly destroyed, its vitality to the life of the city forgotten. We could have walked over the train tracks to reach the river, but I don't think any of us was ever moved to do so.

When the Woman's Building closed in 1991, prey to funding difficulties and changing social priorities, I felt like my civilization had been decimated. I couldn't blame an outside invader; through our labor, women artists gained opportunities to enter mainstream culture and had flooded into galleries and museums. While some of us still believed in the new culture we'd hungered to create, it seemed the historical moment to bring that into being had passed. The inexorable flood of time had overwhelmed its banks and changed the course of everything.

Lauren Bon and her team planted their corn in July of 2005. By Labor Day it was five feet tall. In October that year, I visited the project on a Sunday afternoon. The stalks were over my head. Many people were gathered that afternoon; families with children danced to a drum circle that had assembled.

I could look to the west and see the spires of downtown gleaming from afar, and marvel to find myself in a cornfield in my former backyard. I walked through the corn all the way to the river and stared into its depths. I walked past the red brick structure that had housed the Woman's Building and remembered the future I had once imagined. Artists still rent studio space in the building, but are not working toward any collective purpose.

And what of the land itself? Is it imprinted with the memory of all who have received its bounty? Does it recall the Tongva who understood its rhythms? Does it taste the blood spilled by the succession of conquerors that staked their claim by force? Did the flow of the *zanja* wash away those red stains? Does the land still burn from the iron and steel that thundered over its crust? Does it know the names of the women who re-birthed themselves on this ground? Did it welcome the corn that filled its expanse? Did it pulse to the drum circles of those who gathered to celebrate the return of life?

TERRY
WOLVERTON

The present is nothing like what I once fantasized, yet it is not without its miracles. In 2007, a plan was approved to return the river to its natural state. Perhaps if I live long enough I will see that too, as I have seen the corn harvested, as I have seen the new state park there erupt in wildflowers in spring, bringing a welcome stretch of nature to the steel and concrete of downtown. If I live long enough, who can say what else I might see on this site?

What we experience now we think will be forever, but the land knows this is just a failure of imagination.

"110 Freeway at 105 Freeway"

Celeste Fremon

I lie to people about freeways. I'll give you an example: Friday mornings at around 11 a.m., I leave my Topanga Canyon home and spend two hours driving three Southern California freeways in order to reach the campus of the University of California at Irvine where I teach a weekly writing workshop. Friday afternoons at around 6 p.m., I make the same drive in reverse, except that the afternoon journey is far longer due to the rush-hour traffic. When friends hear of my Topanga to Irvine peregrinations, they regard me with pity. "You poor thing!" they say. "You must hate that drive!"

"Oh, it's not so bad," I reply. I never tell them that, instead of loathing my freeway Fridays, I look forward to the hours spent in the clutches of the 10, the 405, and the 55. I certainly do not admit the deeper truth: that I love our Southern California freeways, a confession I realize is unfashionable in the extreme.

I love the serpentine weaves of concrete for all manner of reasons, but mainly I like them because there's nothing to do on a freeway but drive. In this multitasking world, any period of mono-focus is a blessed time. Freeway driving—even at 6 p.m. on a Friday—is a meditation. Released from the tyranny of productivity, the psyche has room to stretch. One can safely engage in imaginary conversations or follow ideas up irregular trails that may or may not break through into the light. Movement itself—even slow movement in gridlock—is conducive to dreaming.

Sometimes there is the odd mishap. I was once so engrossed in a thought that I *twice* overshot the same exit on the 101. Yet, I suspect, this quality of enforced sensory deprivation is why, despite twenty-five years of hectoring on the part of Caltrans, eighty-six percent of those California residents who travel the freeways to work every day refuse to carpool, a number that even rose slightly from the decade before. They don't want to give up their one oasis of solitary downtime. When one desperately needs a break from the craziness, freeways are the ashram closest at hand.

If we tire of our aloneness, we can also commune. "Let me call you from the road," I say to those friends with whom I long to have an unhurried phone chat, or one of those deeply intimate rambles about everything and nothing that my soul seems regularly to require. Yet, spiritual necessity or no, the category marked "soulful ramble" rarely makes it to a first-tier ranking on my already overcrowded To Do list until an hour stuck in traffic on the 405 affords permission.

I also love our freeways for their iconic quality. There is no architectural element with which Los Angeles County (or Orange County, for that matter) is more closely identified than our 527-plus miles of curves, loops, and straightaways. Manhattan has its skyline, D.C. its monuments, Venice its canals. We've got the four-level interchange. Stealing water from the Owens Valley made metropolitan life in Southern California possible, but the Transportation Engineering Board's Parkway Plan of 1939 shaped it. Los Angeles built the first freeway in the nation, the six-point-five-mile Arroyo Seco Parkway (later renamed the Pasadena), which opened in 1940. But unlike the Parisians, who adore their Eiffel Tower, or San Franciscans, who view the Golden Gate with affection, most Angelenos seem to hate their freeways with an unbridled passion.

We didn't always loathe our übernetwork of roadways. In the 1950s and '60s, when most of the system was built, we considered it a modern marvel. This was in part because L.A. had freeways and other cities didn't. If New Yorkers sniffed at our gauche transportation methods, we simply pointed out that one can't even park in Manhattan, much less drive across town. The red ribbons draped across the county's maps redefined what a metropolis could become. Centralization was no longer required. The future stretched unfettered in all directions every time we rolled down the windows, cranked up the radio, and zoomed without stopping from Hollywood to San Clemente.

Our early freeway boosterism was further abetted by various East Coast and European intellectuals who lauded our multi-miles of cement as the new populist cathedral. In 1960, Charles W. Moore, then dean of the Yale School of Architecture, went so far as to suggest that if one wanted to stage a revolutionary coup in Los Angeles, one would not bother to march on City Hall. "The heart of the city would have to be sought elsewhere," wrote Moore. "The only hope would seem to be to take over the freeways." British design historian Reyner Banham further sanctified our monolithic arteries in 1971 in his quirkily influential book, *Los Angeles: The Architecture of Four*

Ecologies. The freeway speaks the "language of movement, not monument," Banham
trilled. He went on to pronounce that it gave our polymorphous California lifestyle
what it sorely needed, "a comprehensive unity."

By the mid '70s, such cerebral rhapsodizing was giving way to environmental con-
cerns: We were paving paradise at a rapid rate. Construction ground to a halt. It was
still permissible to like freeways, but only if one did so ironically, in the manner of,
say, Joan Didion, who wrote in *Esquire* in 1977 that the freeway driving experience
was "the only secular communion Los Angeles has."

As with a romantic marriage gone bad, much of our current ill will is born of fury at
a pledge that has been rescinded. Reasonable or not, the promise of California had
always been of limitless horizons. The weather was mild, the state was big, the social
stratification of the East was viewed with vague amusement, and for four decades,
the Southern California economy grew as if it were on steroids. Even after loving it
became *démodé*, the freeway system remained a guilty pleasure, a satisfyingly gigantic
metaphor that expressed what we secretly believed to be our geographic superiority.

Then, in the mid-1980s, when the last big population jump exceeded the most opti-
mistic projections of the city's post-World War II planners, freeway driving suddenly
became far less, well, *free*. (In 2007, an average of 325,000 vehicles made their way
down the busiest stretch of the 101 freeway on any given day, a number that is greater
than the entire citizenry of post-Katrina New Orleans.) In other metropolitan areas,
overcrowding might be viewed as an unpleasant but inevitable fact of life. In Los
Angeles, it was seen as a personal impingement, an egregious and wrongful loss of
autonomy and time. All at once, freeways were the enemy. They reduced us to rats
in a maze, people said. They stole our souls, separated us from one another, hijacked
precious hours of our outdoor lives. Angelenos learned they were spending more time
stuck in vehicular gridlock than any other drivers in the nation. We began to worry
that, by driving across town, we were engaging in some kind of collective psychosis
that future historians would parse unpleasantly.

While I am not immune to traffic-caused vexation, the joy offered by the roads
themselves never vanishes. I like the way the Santa Monica births itself into the
sunlight a zillion times a day out of the McClure Tunnel from Pacific Coast Highway, California's mama road. I like the graffiti, painted by high-wire outlaws, that

constantly surprises me from the overpasses. I am still dizzied by the grace of the arched connectors from the Santa Monica to the 405. I love each and every mural. I rejoice at the intense-eyed, bearded guy in Kent Twitchell's mural, *Harbor Freeway Overture*, which looms over the 110 on the parking structure at Citicorp Plaza, and Frank Romero's *Going to the Olympics*, a 103-foot valentine to L.A.'s car culture, which sprawled gloriously along the Hollywood at Alameda, until Caltrans recently and unwisely painted over it.

I also like it that once you get up the on-ramp—any on-ramp—there are fewer decisions to make than down below. I like that people are more polite on the freeway. Yes, there are those drivers on the 101 and the 710 who are too self-absorbed or comatose to let you change lanes, but such incidents are minor when compared with the behavior one finds on Melrose or Victory or Sepulveda. On surface streets, drivers honk over every perceived slight (or no slight at all) with a wrath so murderous, a five-mile drive can leave you twitching for the rest of the day.

I believe that the freeway system is arguably the last best democratic public space in Los Angeles. The use of beaches, parks, and museums tends more and more to fracture along class lines. But on the freeway, unless you're a car pool or a presidential motorcade, nobody gets special treatment. There is no preferred seating, no membership to confer privileges. Short of helicopter service, the only way to get there from here in L.A. County is by taking the 101, the 10, the 5, the 405.

I find it cheering that, day after day, our liquid city is a paella of mothers hauling soccer teams, truckers hauling cantaloupes, pickup laborers hoping for work, attorneys of every possible ethnicity and gender listening to left-and right-leaning talk shows, twentysomethings bumping whatever music moves them, the lone woman (and the occasional man) sobbing over a love song, or maybe singing along—well or poorly. At rush hour, the new Mercedes-Benz S-Class and the primer-covered 1988 Crown Victoria travel at precisely the same speed.

I know it's stylish to speak of freeways as instruments of cultural isolation. Certainly, if one drives from Sherman Oaks to Pomona, one can breeze right by the housing projects of East L.A., as one would flyover states, and never acknowledge their existence. Moreover, freeways were the tool with which the '50s middle-class fantasy of suburbia was made manifest by land barons from the Westside, Palos Verdes, and the Valley out to build their fortunes. Without freeways, white flight would have proved inconvenient.

On the other hand, as a result of freeway construction, the area of land within a thirty-minute drive from L.A.'s civic center leapt from 261 square miles in 1953 to 705 square miles by 1962, a widening of purview that applied equally to anybody with a vehicle and some gas money. Because of freeways, I can make the trip from my house in Topanga to meet friends at our favorite restaurant on 1st Street, east of the river, without ever having to wet my feet, so to speak, in Brentwood, Encino, or Beverly Hills, and my Eastside friends can do the same in reverse.

One last thought: I like freeways because you can scream. If you scream on Wilshire or Burbank or Cesar Chavez Boulevard, bad things are likely to happen. If you scream in your house, the police will show up and require an explanation. On the freeway, no one cares. I first realized this one afternoon in August of 1989, when my then-husband and I decided that, for sure, we were getting a divorce. I suddenly realized this meant that my son, who was four years old at the time, would no longer be sleeping at my house every night, eating the meals I cooked, having me there to keep him safe—joint custody being the price tag of leaving my marriage. The anguish that accompanied this comprehension was so intense, I was sure it would smash me to rubble. So I did the only logical thing: I grabbed my keys and got myself and my Honda Accord onto the Ventura Freeway where, for about twelve miles straight, I screamed and screamed and screamed and screamed.

In the years between then and now I have again let loose at various moments on various freeways. In August of 2002, I screamed in fury and grief on the 405 the day after I got the news that my son's father, my ex, had finally succeeded in drinking himself to death. My boy was drowning in his own anguish at the loss, and I needed to protect him from mine, so I took it to the freeway. I screamed and cried again on the 5 one night in April of 2006 as I drove back from visiting my mother in La Mirada, who spent most of that spring losing dominion over nearly every volitional act except the ability to blink and to breathe.

There were other screaming incidents, each of which brought some measure of comfort. The fact of allowing myself to go temporarily off the rails in the company of strangers, all of us whizzing along side by side in our respective sheet-metal cocoons—alone yet not alone—first wrung me out, then eventually brought me back to ground.

So, yes, I love Southern California's freeways, our profane and sacred concrete pathways of separation and connection. Upon reflection, I'm not one bit sorry about admitting it.

"Carrizo Plain—Western Rattlesnake 10"

David L. Ulin

ETERNITY IN AN HOUR

I used to think the most foreign place I'd ever been was Three Rivers, Texas, a truck stop town about halfway between Corpus Christi and San Antonio, where I worked on a construction crew for a few months at the end of 1979. That, or the country of Romania, which I visited during the Ceausescu era: a through-the-looking-glass panorama of Soviet-style housing blocks and empty boulevards, where the restaurants served cabbage three meals a day. But once I moved to Southern California, I began to realize that foreignness can be found in the most unlikely locations, that it is less a state of being than a state of mind. California, after all—as Walt Whitman once wrote of himself—contains multitudes, and of them, none is quite so foreign as the Carrizo Plain.

The Carrizo Plain is like a Southern California version of the Middle East, a barren expanse of rock and desert that extends north between the Central Valley and the Sierra Madre Mountains, along the jagged spine of the Caliente Range. It looks, I imagine, like Afghanistan or northern Iraq: empty, windswept, sparsely settled, unchanged and unchanging since the dawn of time. Unlike those places, however, you don't need an expeditionary force to visit the Carrizo; all you have to do is drive seventy-five miles north on I-5 from Los Angeles, exiting at the mountain town of Frazier Park, near the crest of Tejon Pass. From there, it's a quick jaunt through the northeast corner of Los Padres National Forest down to the town of Maricopa, where the Carrizo spreads out like a geographic question mark. Twenty miles north, the Temblor Range cuts the vista with its looping curves and chasms, rocky hillsides slit with scar-like gullies where the earth has pulled apart. Off to the west, Soda Lake dots the horizon in a glossy comma, heat waves shimmering off its surface in wisps of gauze. Pull off the road, walk back from the shoulder fifteen, even ten feet, and it's like no road has ever existed, like there's nothing here at all. This is about as far as you can get from Los Angeles—not just in Southern California, but anywhere—a blank slate, a terrain of imagination, of possibility and terror, of abiding fear and awe.

When I use words like awe and terror, I'm not being hyperbolic, although I don't mean it as a negative. Rather, what the Carrizo offers, even for an instant, is a way to step back from civilization, to get in touch with our more essential selves. In this too, I'd suggest, it's like the Middle East, the Middle East of the Koran, of the Old Testament, where everywhere, it seems, you feel the presence of God. Partly, that has to do with the Carrizo's seismic legacy; it's the best spot in California to come face-to-face with the San Andreas Fault, which cuts the rocky plain floor like an attenuated seam. Once, at Wallace Creek, where over the last four millennia, the San Andreas has put a four hundred-plus foot dogleg into a formerly straight streambed, I climbed down into the fault trace and waited for an earthquake; the last time this segment ruptured, in 1857, the surface slip measured thirty-one feet. It's impossible to stand here and not be reminded of your insignificance, a feeling heightened by the Carrizo's wildness: the stone and wind and emptiness, the silence and the sky. In such a landscape, time becomes elastic, open-ended, as if we had somehow walked out into eternity itself. This may sound contradictory—insignificance on the one hand and eternity on the other—but that's the beauty of the Carrizo, the way it forces us to look beyond our preconceptions and confront the complications of a starkly elemental world.

Of course, as with everything in California, the Carrizo is hardly as unspoiled as it once was, and the further east you go, the more contemporary life creeps in. Yet here as well, it's a peculiar kind of contemporary life—rough, unpolished, with many of its seams exposed. On Highway 33, which runs south from Coalinga before bottoming out past Maricopa, Amoco and Chevron have built enormous oil fields that stretch back from both sides of the road. At their most extensive, just north of McKittrick, the wells reach to the horizon, thousands of them pumping, moving to their own slow rhythm like mechanical birds. Pickups rumble past as men in hardhats check pipelines that wind out of the fields to front the road. For another moment, on this stretch of blacktop, you might imagine yourself in the Middle East again, although a more secular Middle East this time, the strategic region where we wage our wars. Then, you pull into McKittrick, with its 1930s-era red-brick hotel and its general store. And just like that, you're back in California, in the alien territory of the Carrizo Plain.

Scott Timberg

COOL GUY WITH A CAMERA: AN APPRECIATION
*The unobtrusive photographer William Claxton was just as hip
as the musicians he helped immortalize.*

OCTOBER 21, 2008

It's been a tough few weeks for West Coast geniuses. Still reeling from the death of David Foster Wallace, I was startled to see that photographer Bill Claxton passed away on Oct. 11, the day before his 81st birthday.

In the nearly 20 years I've been writing about culture, rarely have I met a guy as unimpeachably cool as Claxton. He didn't do anything as radical as reimagine the literary novel, as Wallace did. But he proved that genuinely talented artists are far more humble and easy to get along with than the larger numbers of hustlers and second-raters. That, I imagine, is because they are both secure and open, from spending time with people who play at their level.

Claxton's most important contribution was, in the words of author Ted Gioia, "creating the mystique of West Coast jazz." At a time when East Coast critics either ignored or condescended to cool jazz, Claxton created a new visual reality recognized even by people with little knowledge of music.

That reality was very different than the way New York jazz was usually represented. "The musicians were always perspiring," Claxton told me once, with a laugh. "I said to myself, 'It's not like that out here.' "

In his shots, "they played at the beach, they wore Hawaiian shirts, there was sunlight everywhere."

A decade ago, when he was having a renaissance, I spent some time with Claxton for a story. Though his fame had mostly come in the 1950s, he was so busy (and fairly absent-minded) that it took me months to get my first interview.

As a teenager, Claxton told me, he had invited Charlie Parker to his parents' house in La Canada after a show on Central Avenue. ("Did you give him something to eat?" his mother asked.)

He talked about discovering Chet Baker's striking looks only in his photographs, after being unimpressed with the trumpeter in person. "It has nothing to do with how beautiful you are," Claxton said. "A lot of it has to do with how you project emotionally. I know it sounds mysterious, but it's true."

Images like Claxton's famous shot of Baker brooding into the top of a piano —the cover of the "Let's Get Lost" album—captured not only the musician's offhand, slightly dandified beauty but his unrelieved narcissism. Claxton talked about Baker as being mostly "passive" with men, dependent with women and spoiled rotten with both.

The photographer's own presence was very different. "I'm such an awful tall guy that if they didn't get used to me, I'd be a terrible annoyance," he said of his subjects. "I kind of blend into the background. They think I'm another mike stand."

Claxton described returning to Los Angeles in the 1970s, after living in New York and Europe, and finding the city vastly more aggressive, more selfish, than he remembered.

He talked about how the music industry had changed with the invasion of lawyers, handlers and security goons who made it impossible to spend real time with an artist and improvise a portrait.

In the 1990s, he became a father figure to Benedikt Taschen and hung out at the John Lautner house in which the publisher then lived. There, Claxton would bump into "Billy Wilder, a porn star, a few writers, someone who'd worked with Andy Warhol, saxophonist Benny Carter. After a semiformal dinner, the evening would burst into a dance party. Benedikt would play jazz and dance on the table. Everybody would dance, including his chef."

One of his descriptions struck me as a truism of the artistic process in general. "My technique is no secret," he said. "I try to spend as much time as possible with a person before I shoot them. I usually get to know their fears."

My favorite photo of his is probably of Art Pepper, saxophone slung under his arm, walking up a hill in Echo Park, a West Coast Sisyphus. Claxton told me Pepper had just gotten out of jail the day before and was waiting in Echo Park to score heroin but was jumpy because he'd cut his hand on a soup can.

As with Claxton's shot of John Coltrane earnestly ascending a staircase, the more you know about the men and their music, the more eloquent the photographs are.

Claxton survived an era that all but destroyed Baker, Pepper and others. Some of his most expressive shots have nothing to do with the Cool School: Ornette Coleman looking lanky and awkward on the cover of "The Shape of Jazz to Come," Sonny Rollins in a cowboy hat in "Way Out West," Thelonious Monk on a cable car (Claxton had to take the pianist for a drink in North Beach first) for "Alone in San Francisco."

Claxton, of course, shot much more than jazz. His most famous photograph is likely the one of his wife, Peggy Moffitt, posing in Rudi Gernreich's topless swimsuit. His outside work ranges from the sublime—killer pictures of Elvis Costello and Burt Bacharach for the "Painted From Memory" CD—to the ridiculous, directing what he considered was some terrible TV.

He was the kind of guy everyone wants to have on their team, so he's likely to be claimed by fashion people, Hollywood types, Steve McQueen obsessives and others.

When I asked him 10 years ago how he thought he would be remembered, he was unambiguous. "I think I'm so deeply rooted in jazz," he said, "that it'll say on my tombstone that I was a jazz photographer."

Silver Lake

Golden State Fwy.

L.A. River

Effie St.

Police Acdmy

Boylston St.

Solano Ave.

Dodger Stadium

Elysian Park Ave.

Naval Armory

Chavez Ravine Rd.

No. Broadway

Pasadena Fw.

"Dodger Stadium"

Benjamin & Christina Schwarz

DODGER STADIUM, LOS ANGELES

Dodger Stadium is best from its cheapest seats. From there, at the rim of the Chavez Ravine, the players are too small to distract you from the view of the green-and-gold Elysian Hills, fading to blue in the sunset. What makes this vista beguiling makes Los Angeles as a whole winning: whimsical artificiality set against natural grandeur. A straight line of tall, absurdly skinny palms strings across the closest ridge, and a soda-pop-orange Union 76 ball appears to float among them—magically, a scene charming rather than vulgar. Seemingly just beyond these trees, and beyond the Police Academy's idyllic Spanish-style, eucalyptus-laced campus, loom the San Gabriel Mountains, among the most abruptly rising in the world and sometimes still snowcapped on opening day. In the other direction, out past the Dodger Dog stand, the whole of downtown, Art Deco to postmodern, appears smack at eye level, behind a grove of ficus trees, with their dense, vibrant-green, broccoli-like crowns. Some people hate Los Angeles because they perceive it to be artificial, but perched at the top of Dodger Stadium, you can see the city's art. L.A. has taken nature and made it better.

"Panoramic View, Chavez Ravine"

"Valley Blvd. Sign"

Denise Hamilton

SAN GABRIEL VALLEY—AMERICA'S FIRST SUBURBAN CHINATOWN

As a reporter for the *Los Angeles Times*, I was lucky enough to cover the collapse of Communism in Eastern Europe. When I returned to L.A., everything seemed pale and insipid by comparison. Even worse, the paper assigned me to a bureau far from Moscow or Berlin.

They sent me to the San Gabriel Valley.

I'd have preferred Siberia. The Valley was one big ur-suburb, crammed with light industry, malls and tract homes. The pastel map grids of *Les Frères Thomas* listed towns like Covina, Duarte, Alhambra, El Monte, Pomona and Azusa. I'd often hurtled past them on the freeway, bound for somewhere else. Now they would be my destination.

This was not the L.A. that I knew and cherished, the worlds so vividly drawn by James Cain, Nathanael West and Joan Didion. This was not the L.A. of Steven Spielberg or David Hockney or Wolfgang Puck. This was a landscape far, far east of La Brea. Nobody power-lunched in the San Gabriel Valley. They were too busy working to pay off the second mortgage on those cookie-cutter homes.

Our office lay halfway to San Bernardino in a city called Monrovia and shared space in a bleak shopping center with Toys R Us and Mervyn's. By 9 a.m. on summer mornings, the bony spines of the San Gabriel Mountains to the north would be obscured by a thick brown haze. They were a scrubby and desolate range from which bears and mountain lions emerged regularly to confront hillside residents. Each year, flash floods and icy ridges in the Angeles National Forest killed several people. We were so close to the city, but nature, too, demanded its pound of flesh. It was only we who called it accidents.

In the dead space between interviews and board meetings, I cruised the Valley's wide avenues. Whenever possible, I grilled cops, teachers, business owners, and social workers about my new stomping grounds. But it was a realtor who taught me about the "Golden Triangle," the heavily Asian communities of Hacienda Heights, Rowland Heights and Walnut that clustered around the Hsi Lai Buddhist Temple at the base of the foothills.

Here, big American developers wouldn't dream of breaking ground until their *feng shui* consultant vetted the land and signed off on the blueprints. Here, every blond sales agent knew her business phone ended with triple eight because that meant good luck in Chinese numerology. Here, Latino workmen were adept at installing built-in stovetop woks and storage cupboards for fifty-pound bags of rice.

One day a cop invited me on a brothel raid and I joined agents from the FBI, INS, L.A. County sheriff and local detectives as they broke down the doors of three suburban tract houses where teenaged Asian girls smuggled across the Pacific were forced to work as sex slaves to pay off their $35,000 passage. There, I found a poem on crumpled paper in the trash that a *Chinese Daily News* reporter translated for me. It read in part:

> *Please let me forget about this*
> *And give me one night without sorrow*
> *Let me go through rain and wind*
> *Until I see my home again*
> *Maybe I will drink to ease this heavy heart*
> *But you will never see me shed a tear*

On a brighter note, I also found the San Gabriel Village Square, an anomaly that only the Pacific Rim fantasy aesthetic of Los Angeles could have produced. Built in a Spanish Mission style, with dusky peach tones, the three-story shopping center served the overseas Chinese community. On occasion, a looky-loo gringa like myself would wander through, but we were the exception.

Here, you could gorge on Islamic Chinese food, buy designer suits from Hong Kong, pick out live lobsters and $700 bottles of French cognac and take out a $1 million insurance policy on your cheating spouse. I half-expected to see Jackie Chan hurtling off the balcony of the Ranch 99 market wearing his trademark grin, with scar-faced, gun-wielding gangsters in hot pursuit.

Eventually, this shopping center came to symbolize the changes racing through the San Gabriel Valley like a major earthquake. In the late 1980s, Monterey Park became the first continental U.S. city with a majority Asian population. Tradition-

ally WASPy enclaves such as San Marino are now half Asian, as is master-planned
Walnut on the region's eastern rim. Drive along Valley Boulevard, the main Asian
commercial thoroughfare, and you'll see as many signs in Chinese as English. Many
wealthy and middle-class immigrants now bypass traditional Chinatown altogether,
making the San Gabriel Valley the nation's first suburban Chinatown.

1   Spare Ribs w/Chili &
    Black Bea
    剁椒蒸排骨
3   Steamed B.B.Q. Pork Bun
    蠔汁叉燒飽
1   Golden Cream Bun
    至尊流沙飽
1   Shrimp Stuff w/Baby Green
    百花娃娃菜
    Shanghai Style Steamd Bun
    上海小鸄包

"This Receipt Is Wonderful"

There is a historic continuum to all this that strikes me as inevitable. Hadn't the
peaceful and nomadic Gabrieleno Indians been swept away 150 years earlier by gold
miners and Spanish land grantees, whose beautiful daughters were in turn assimi-
lated through marriage with WASP pioneers from the Eastern Seaboard?

One sweltering day when the heat rising from the asphalt was enough to trigger
hallucinations, I realized I was as much a foreign correspondent here as I had been in
Central Europe, and that's exactly how I should cover it. My turf began just 10 miles
east of downtown, but light years removed from the monolithic towers of corporate
America. With its 1.3 million residents, the Valley was a bubbling brew of new im-

migrants and old-timers, small business and multi-million dollar shopping centers. All the big West Coast cities were morphing into 21st century Pacific Rim capitals, but in the San Gabriel Valley, the future had already here. If this place had an ethos, it was "Welcome, stranger. Come live among us and prosper."

With apologies to Ridley Scott's *Blade Runner* and Philip K. Dick, I believe the future of Los Angeles lies not in the claustrophobic urban core, but in the suburbs where the last empty spaces of the wild, wild west meet and fuse with an even wilder East.

It's a world that's slowly seeping into American letters and cinema. If Raymond Chandler were writing today, he'd send Philip Marlowe to investigate the murder of a Hong Kong businessman who left behind a beautiful wife, a mistress and an Irwindale factory that made silicon chips worth their weight in gold. The Midwestern extras who yearned for Hollywood oblivion in Nathanael West's *Day of the Locust* would be recast as survivors of Pol Pot's killing fields living above a Cambodian eatery in Alhambra. And Joan Didion might hunker down in a Monterey Park nightclub with Hong Kong's bicultural "golden youth."

My own journey into fiction began the day as I stood in front of a huge Tudor house in San Marino. It was the type of place that a successful bank president might own. Instead, two teenagers lived here on their own.

They were part of a widespread phenomenon called "parachute kids." Typically, the entire family parachuted in from Hong Kong, Seoul, or Taipei to establish a foothold in the U.S. as a hedge against political or economic uncertainty at home. The parents bought a house in an affluent neighborhood, enrolled the kids in school, then jetted back to Asia (the dads were called astronauts) to oversee family businesses. Some left behind nannies or an auntie but the kids I ended up calling Jonathan, eighteen, and his sister Zoe, fourteen, were alone, unless you counted the elderly Chinese housekeeper who didn't speak English. Parenting was done electronically and when Dad visited L.A. on business.

"We've been on our own so long that we really don't know what it's like to have parents," Jonathan told me, staring at two large screen TVs. One was tuned to a Chinese satellite channel. The other to MTV. Just like the two lobes of his brain, I thought, wondering whether he ever heard static as the circuits crossed.

Later, a youth counselor at a Rosemead clinic told me that alienation, lack of parenting and loneliness ate away at youngsters like Jonathan. Most avoided trouble but others joined Asian youth gangs like the Wah Ching, the V Boys or the Black Dragons, working as hired muscle for older gangsters from the Chinese triads. Parents sitting in safe old Taipei had no idea of the scary stuff lurking in our upscale American suburbs. The neighborhoods might look like movie sets, but when trouble went down it was a John Woo movie, not *American Graffiti*. Guns and no roses, and 1,001 ways for a kid to go bad, when he's sixteen and hurting.

I wrote a long piece for the *Times* about Jonathan and Zoe, but it didn't satisfy me. I chafed at the limitations of journalism. I wanted to crawl inside their heads, imagine what happened to them and their friends long after I had filed my story and gone home.

Each night, the voices of the San Gabriel Valley replayed like a broken tape loop in my brain, clicking and whirring in a multitude of languages. They were the voices of fear, resignation and hope. A microcosm of our society. A glimpse into an unwieldy future. Soon after that, I started writing fiction.

Shark: 32 feet long, Weight 7 ton or 14000 lbs.
Caught by Peter Borcich of San Pedro, California.

"32 Foot Long Shark"

Jenny Price

Thirteen Ways of Seeing Nature in L.A.

"This is a happy land for children and all young animals . . . They live in the pure air and sunshine."
—*Health Seekers' [and] Tourists' . . . Guide to the . . . Pacific Coast*, 1884

"The palm trees were high with scrawny fronds like broken pinwheels . . . and a droopy ice plant could never quite hold the earth . . . in place . . . and an oil derrick [looked] like a rusty praying mantis, trying to suck the last few barrels out of the dying crabgrass."
—Robert Towne, on researching his 1974 *Chinatown* script

"And waiting in the wings are the plague squirrels and killer bees."
—Mike Davis, *Ecology of Fear*, 1998

"Experience the beauty . . . of another culture while learning more about wastewater treatment and reuse."
—Brochure for the combination water reclamation plant and Japanese garden in the San Fernando Valley, 2002

L.A., like no other city, has woven nature stories thoroughly into stories about the city itself. From the nineteenth-century boosters to the popular Land of Sunshine magazine in the early 1900s to Raymond Chandler and Nathanael West in the 1930s and '40s to Didion to Mike Davis to the current coverage in the *Los Angeles Times* and *New York Times*, L.A.'s interpreters have been obsessed with sea, sun, winds, sky, and palm trees, as well as fire, mud, earthquakes, plague squirrels, and killer bees.

And even Davis, from whom I have learned so much about how to see Los Angeles, imagines nature in opposition to cities.

Consider the American dream and nightmare stories. To simplify egregiously, these dominant L.A. narratives really parse into three kinds of tales—dream, nightmare, and apocalypse—that have coexisted since at least the 1930s but have progressed roughly in dominance, in that order. In the beginning, L.A. was the American Eden: it was the land of eternal sunshine, healthful sea breezes, and amazingly fertile soils. The late-nineteenth-century boosters lauded the virtues of wild nature to market L.A. as a sort of non-city city. L.A. was supposed to be an Anglo refuge where you could escape the industrial pollution, ethnic and racial conflicts, and financial disappointments in cities to the east—and the ensuing dream stories would continue to use fabulous paeans to sun and sea and air to frame idyllic visions of urban escape, from the post–World War II garden suburbs to today's canyon living in Malibu and the Hollywood Hills.

And then, the nightmare: the black sky, the fouled sea, the endless pavement, the dying palm trees, the concrete river. By the 1960s, as L.A. defaults on its promises of escape and pushes the problems of American cities to extremes, the Paradise Lost tales invariably invoke the utter destruction of nature to describe a city in which everything has gone wrong. And after the nightmare, the millennium: "Is the City of Angels Going to Hell?" *Time* asks in a 1993 cover story. In the early 1990s, L.A. reels from the Northridge earthquake, Malibu fires, mudslides, race riots, El Niño, and the O. J. Simpson trial. And the city that destroyed nature and everything else becomes the city where nature roared back for revenge. Apocalypse stories make the opposition of nature to cities decidedly literal.

The history of L.A. storytelling, if more complicated, still basically boils down to a trilogy. Nature blesses L.A. Nature flees L.A. And nature returns armed.

In other words, no wonder I love L.A. This city has been hosting an obsessive conversation about nature for 150 years—or about as far back as when Thoreau camped out on Walden Pond. Nature stories have been more than key L.A. stories. They've been *the* L.A. stories. It's ironic, isn't it? Los Angeles, which symbolizes the city as anti-nature, really has long flourished as a mecca for thinking and writing about nature, and for telling this powerful story, in particular, that nature writing has so dedicatedly perpetuated.

Which makes perfect sense, if you think about it. In the modern United States, as in any human society, the stories we tell about nature are the most basic stories we can tell. L.A. has long been a place where we articulate grand American narratives. So it should not surprise us either that the foundational L.A. story is, what?—a nature story—or that we've told a wildly evasive nature tale to describe a city that's pushed the evasion of accountability to people and nature to an extreme. The dream tales have assured us that L.A. is a city of nature where you can escape the social and environmental troubles of cities. The destruction of nature in the nightmare tales—how can you fix something that no longer exists?—laments the city's troubles while assuring us that we don't have to do anything because the problems are beyond repair. And how much further past salvation could a city be that awaits imminent millennial annihilation by nature? Here is a city where we've dreamt brilliantly of virtue while doing spectacularly unvirtuous things. It practically vibrates with brilliant denial in the service of spectacular yearning, self-interest, and material indulgence. And the city's definitive story is a way of seeing nature that allows for and encourages these exact evasions.

What we need in L.A., as elsewhere, is a foundational literature that imagines nature not as the opposite of the city but as the basic stuff of modern everyday life. We could use a great deal less "And waiting in the wings are the plague squirrels and killer bees," and a lot more tales that explore our daily, intertwined connections to nature and to each other—such as "Enjoy the beauty of another culture while learning more about wastewater treatment and reuse."

I love that L.A. has been a uniquely powerful place to tell American nature stories. But as long as L.A. has been a mecca for American stories, writers have been calling for new stories with which to see the city. And nature stories have to be the logical place to start.

"View of Plaza Church"

D. J. Waldie

The house of God and the gate of heaven
From the old plaza church to the cathedral on the hill

1.

A pilgrim, you come out of the ground beneath Union Station to stand in the cathedral-like space of the waiting room, layered over with its recollections of a Hollywood version of a Latino past. And you go through the bronze doors of the waiting room to face the old plaza where that past in this city began. The summer light is as hard and gray as if reflected from a high wall of concrete. You cross Alameda Street and walk up the hill into the city's contested heart—a place no less reworked to be a metaphor. There is a church there, on the west side of the old Plaza, the city's first church—*Nuestra Señora la Reina de los Angeles*, the Our Lady Queen of the Angels.

You pass through the small, noisy, and profoundly human courtyard on the north side of the Plaza church—where it smells of *tacos al carbon* being grilled, burning candle wax, and the pomade of bridegrooms—and turn left on Spring Street, climbing higher now, across the canyon of the 101 Freeway and up Temple Street through the blind acropolis of government buildings, to the foot of the promontory on which rises (behind its repellent perimeter wall) the city's new cathedral. It, too, is dedicated to Our Lady of the Angels.

I'm Catholic and, I suppose, one of the faithful. I've worshipped in both the plaza church and the new cathedral, stepped forward in both to receive what I understand to be divine flesh, felt something in both that I imagined to be grace, and examined there all the longings that bring me back.

On this Sunday, the congregants gathering for Mass—indistinguishable from tourists and architecture students—climb the steps from the street level gate to stand at the southeastern edge of the platform on which the vermillion walls of the cathedral rise. Everything, except for a green row of palms and a little grove of olive trees, is the color of California hills after a year of drought. The concrete reverberates with dun colored light. It's a relief to enter through the black mouth of Robert Graham's bronze doors into a tunnel, rising and narrowing ahead, where the light, passed through a band of translucent alabaster and then half reflected from the yellow limestone floor, is the color of tarnished gold. The corridor pulls me and the other congregants upward toward a semi-ruined baroque *reredo*—an altar screen twisting with traditional Catholic imagery—that marks the summit of the cathedral hill and the turn from the tunnel's semi-darkness into the non-judgmental light falling into the pool of the baptistery and the reticent space of the nave below.

The Cathedral of Our Lady of the Angels is not so much a mud-colored building as it is a specific volume of yellowish light. This light does not play across interior surfaces in the way that light through stained glass animates the figures of cherubs and martyrs in a more sentimental cathedral. When the gray overcast thickens outside, the tone of the light inside changes wholly, miraculously, and everywhere at once.

2.

Whatever symbol of power or metaphor of faith a cathedral might be, it's also something of a machine for praying. On this Sunday, even after many visits, I still haven't learned how to use its spiritual technology—its lack of right angles, the patterns in its concrete that are so much like skin, and, most of all, the untouchable authority claimed by its light. I don't know what prayers the cathedral and I are saying together yet; I don't think many of my fellow believers do.

Some of them scatter in silence to the rows of cherrywood pews; some move closer to John Nava's tapestries hung against the walls of the nave; and some—propelled by the fabric of the cathedral—continue to the bottom of the nave and up the steps of the sanctuary, past the vast altar table (the color of drying blood), to the crucifix just behind and raised slightly above.

Secular commentary on the cathedral has dwelled on its abstraction, more Zen than Catholic, and emphasized how understated are matters of faith in the building's structure. The secular commentators didn't stay for what happens next. For pilgrims journeying through the cathedral, the end of the journey is Simon Toparovsky's life-size bronze figure of a man, black skin flayed, nailed up to a post. Nothing subdued or Zen-like there, nothing sentimental, no appeal to a consoling immigrant Catholic experience of community and folk piety. It isn't possible to be nostalgic about crucifixion.

The worshippers who have gathered around the crucifix reach out to the feet and knees of the dark figure and touch them tentatively. Some boldly lean in to kiss the metal that's losing its iron oxide patina. Their embraces are taking away sacredness and making it theirs.

3.

During the sermon, the servers bring out a large brazier to illustrate a point the priest is making about prayer. He pours a handful of incense onto the coals until the flames drive up a wide column of light grey smoke. I anticipate that the cloying odor of burning incense—a powerful instigator of Catholic memories—will fill the air. It doesn't. By an accident of geometry or ventilation, the cloud ascends, spreads into a veil, and joins the light, but the burning incense leaves no smell.

Architect José Rafael Monéo's design for the cathedral has a way of sustaining these contradictions and leaving then unresolved. That equipoise hung in the air and light on this particular Sunday until the moment of consecration in the Canon of the Mass when a large disk of pale tan bread was held up as high as the young, slightly affected priest could reach above the altar, and all the contradictions and lack of resolution in Moneo's design didn't matter.

Bread and wine turning into body and blood is better left to the Catholic imagination, which doesn't require this building. This building, with its $195-million cost and impact on the ability of the archdiocese to serve its community, will continue to feel like an outsized act of one man's will long after Cardinal Mahony's crimson cardinal's hat—by custom hung after a cardinal's death from the rafters of his cathedral—joins the hats of Cardinals Manning and McIntyre, already relocated from other churches and suspended high in the cathedral's indifferent light.

"The Mass is ended," the brutally over-amplified voice of the priest tells us. The choir sings a last hymn.

The way back takes us past Cardinal Mahony's hastily dedicated "chapel of the abused children," one of ten unfinished bays in the fifty-foot-high screen wall around the nave. The chapel was the cardinal's gesture in 2003 to the mothers and fathers of the children molested by diocesan priests since the 1960s.

In the chapel, color photographs of smiling young faces are stapled to the framework of a wooden cross. A cheerful, incongruous banner left over from the cathedral's dedication decorates the rear wall. A condolence book, as if for a funeral, is propped up on a small table. The book's opening pages are burdened with messages of bitterness and anger from parents at what had happened to their sons and daughters. Later pages have been appropriated for prayers to Our Lady, an appeal by a loving granddaughter for the health of her grandfather, and requests for similar blessings.

(The chapel has since been dismantled.)

We pass into the everyday light outside, to cross the desert of the cathedral plaza, to descend its hill. Below is the church of Our Lady Queen of Angels, rebuilt so many times since 1822 that its simplicity is as abstract as the new cathedral's sophisticated critique of modernism. There are older churches and churches more self-consciously historic. The plaza church wasn't a mission, like San Gabriel or San Fernando. Not much of it is original, except the part it plays in the life of the city. On Saturdays and Sundays particularly—when crowds attending baptisms and weddings spill into the courtyard outside the north entrance—the little church, familiarly called La Placita, is a place of passionate, sacred noise.

Inside, the afternoon light is watery green and somber. A couple is walking up the short, dark aisle toward the bright, gilded *reredo* that frames the altar. In the shallow bay on the left is a painting of the Virgin of Guadalupe. Pinned to a bulletin board are wounded snapshots, each picture pleading for solace or some grace to endure. Lying in a glass case is a life-size sculpture of the crucified body of a very Castilian Jesus, its wood and plaster painted a naïve white over which the greenish pallor of death has been applied.

4.

La Placita and the cathedral, two churches named in honor of Our Lady of the Angels and at the center of the city's divided, Catholic heart. One church holds a pale god; the other a dark one. One church is rooted in the city; the other rises over it. One has been molded by the hands of believers for nearly 200 years; the other is aloof, but that is changing. Imperfect faith will lead us one day to reconcile what is sacred in both.

A significantly different version of this California journey was published in the *Los Angeles Times* Opinion section in August 2003. Another version was collected in *Where We Are Now: Notes from Los Angeles* (published by Angel City Press) in 2004.

"Coyote in the Road, Kelso, California 09.15.2007"

Deanne Stillman

KADDISH FOR A COYOTE

I'm not sure exactly when it was that Brother Coyote first called me to the desert. The master trickster and once-and-future shaman and deliverer of all news funny and tragic is behind all manner of events and moments. Sometimes I think it was when I had a vision of my grandmother handing me a vial of water—my own tears, I realized a few moments later—at a rocky shrine under a mighty Joshua tree. Other times I have ascribed it to DNA or spiritual coding, and then sometimes, I think that it's all about Van Halen, because the only place you can hear them any more is on jukeboxes in desert bars, or in your own car on your own CD and the best way to listen to them is driving fast across a desert two-lane, which is when you might actually see a coyote, if you can slow down without flipping your car before he vanishes.

For a long time, I was exploring the desert east of Los Angeles, the Mojave and Colorado deserts that are encompassed by Joshua Tree National Park and beyond. Then I met the photographer Mark Lamonica, who, after exploring the Los Angeles River for many years and memorializing the local Ganges in *Rio L.A.* with writer Patt Morrison, had established a new outpost in the Antelope Valley, whose vast, flat emptiness provided solitude and relief from urban travail. After learning of my simpatico with the Joshua tree, he told me he had one in his backyard.

As it turned out, he was a bit of a coyote himself, for the tree was across the street. But no matter; since then we have driven and hiked and climbed the paths and byways of L.A.'s least-talked-about valley and discovered an amazing story, one that connects Los Angeles to itself. It began with another message from Brother Coyote. "It's time for a visit to the Devil's Punchbowl," he said. "Go now." The Devil's Punchbowl is a deep and stunning abyss in the San Andreas Fault. Mike Davis once referred to the Antelope Valley as "the virgin bride"; I like to think of the

Punchbowl as the womb of Los Angeles County. You can hike down into it, and I have, many times, even under a full moon.

Mark pointed his Mustang for the Punchbowl and we headed north through the San Gabriels and then turned off on to the 138, aka Tweaker Highway, and all manner of other names that warn motorists of doom. Then we followed the signs for the Devil. As you shall see, there is nothing to fear. Mark remained with the mascot raptors at the ranger station, an owl and a hawk that had been injured and greeted visitors from the large enclosures that were their home. Heeding the call of Brother Coyote, I ventured into the womb of the virgin bride, sacred vessel of all there is and has ever been, past pinyon and juniper and down the narrowing incline, as the sun's rays danced across the granite walls which glittered in response. Some leaves rustled in the lower elevations and a bobcat ran from the scrub. This was, after all, his domain. I continued to the bottom and soon reached the very center of the center of Los Angeles (apologies to those who have situated it elsewhere)—a mounded rock around which a trickle of water flowed, hinting at the stream which gallops through the bowl after the monsoons, the very liquid which the first nations followed all the way to the ocean. I sat down, folded my legs, and listened. From the distance, there came one of the periodic sonic booms from Edwards. Then it was quiet again—there were no sounds of civilization; no suck-and-whine of Harley pipes, no huffing diesels, no pings or rings or horns. Then the silence became even more pronounced, and all I could hear was my breathing, and after a while I began to hear my own blood coursing through my body—a sound that is familiar to me after many desert sojourns, but nonetheless overwhelming, like the immense Tibetan *ohmmmmm* of an onrushing wave at a rocky break.

What do you have to tell me these days? I asked the bowl, for that's how we usually began. Whither Los Angeles? To quote the Clash, should I stay or should I go? And then I waited, because waiting is the way of the desert and I knew the answer might not come quickly. The sun rose higher in the sky and no message was forthcoming—only the sound of my own life force continuing on its way. I sat with the mounded rock for a length of time and realized, as the sun approached high noon, that there was no answer to be had that day, or any day, although for one quick moment, I thought I heard "Dust in the Wind," or maybe it was my ancestors chanting, and then I saw an image of Sacajawea, or perhaps it was Janis Joplin, or maybe even the eternal hitchhiker on the side of the road, or maybe it was a shape-shifting mountain lion, because that's why the Indians called it the Devil's Punchbowl. In any case, the image vanished before I could discern its name, and from nature's broadcasting station came nothing more, if indeed the image had actually materialized in the first place. Sometimes that too is the way of the desert—you can wait forever and it throws you a curve, leaving you to your own epiphanies or demons, forcing you—that skank!—to answer your own questions. I hiked out of the stone chalice, a tough climb with a steep grade, and was now very hungry.

Back on the 138, we headed for a favorite desert pit stop: The Country Mart in the town of Pearblossom. We parked and raced in for the best egg salad sandwiches west of the Mississippi. The Country Mart is a classic Mojave store. It stocks propane, tat mags, sleds in the winter, motocross goggles, and all manner of packaged jerky. As we waited in line to pay, a ringtone went off. It was "I Drink Alone" by George Thorogood, and a guy in a mullet answered his phone as the lyric "Me and my buddy weiser" trailed off into the store chatter. It was the best ringtone I had ever heard, and one that you would never hear in the lower elevations. I gave the guy a nod and we sat down in front of the wood-burning stove and ate our sandwiches.

On the way back to L.A., we heard one more time from Brother Coyote. He was lying on the road at call box 138-62, the latest victim of Death Alley. He had been hit by a car, or so it seemed, for a leg was broken. When it happened we could not tell, but he was stiff, and in the high desert winds, the kind that knocks big rigs to their sides and strips paint from cars and makes it impossible to make flame no matter how you cup your hands or in which direction you face, his beautiful pelt riffled. I ran my hands through his coat and said Kaddish, and he still seemed to have that coyote grin, with his teeth bared and now forever exposed to the elements. Mark moved him to the scrub where Caltrans wouldn't find him but the ravens would, and said "R.I.P., my friend." I thought of an old Mary Austin story, the one called "The Last Antelope," about a hunter and coyote who vied to take down the region's last one, and it was the hunter who got to him first, but his shot also felled the coyote, and as the hunter mourned the episode, coyotes appeared from nowhere and gorged on the antelope carcass. Now, as we headed back to the car, there came another coyote, perhaps the mate of the felled coyote, for they travel in pairs, and it watched us merge back into traffic, maybe guiding us, and it continued watching us, and we it, until we could see each other no longer.

This piece appeared in the *LA City Beat* February 7, 2008.

Thomas Curwen

In the Shadow of the San Gabriels

One August morning in 1877, John Muir went for a walk. Armed with three loaves of bread and some tea, he headed northwest out of Pasadena, soon coming upon a long, dry wash littered with flood boulders and overshadowed by the towering San Gabriel Mountains.

Muir penned his account of his excursion—ostensibly a survey of the bee colonies in California during a drought year—in *The Mountains of California*, and it is our first account of the urban wilderness that surrounds Los Angeles, a place already checkered, as he wrote, "with brusque little bits of civilization."

That Muir would deign to spend time in Southern California and its chaparral-studded mountains might surprise us today, but the bearded sage of the Sierra never met a range he didn't like.

If only it were as easy nowadays, but the mountains of Southern California—a crescent, really, running from Santa Barbara to Mexico—are often difficult to love. More nemesis than tonic to our lives, they turn to mud in the winter, bake under the thermal inversions of our summer and ignite in the fall. Nor are they the most spectacular range in the state, and they are easily diminished by the magnetic hold of Los Angeles, our perpetually self-interested city. Accordingly, we drive through them, seldom pausing, on our way to the more regal splendors of the High Sierra.

But their pleasures abound. Of the 4,083 square miles of Los Angeles County, almost half—1,875 square miles—is mountainous, and the trails that run through make up a civic network as grand and as significant to the life of this city as its artistic, cultural and sporting organizations. Privileged to have the Music Center, Walt Disney Concert Hall, the Getty and LACMA, we are no less fortunate for the unpaved world that surrounds us.

After spending his first night in the company of an amiable, perhaps garrulous homesteader who imparted his hopes of planting an orange grove and a vineyard not far from the reaches of the canyon, Muir continued the next morning deeper into the canyon, soon coming upon a waterfall "singing like a bird, as it pours from a notch in a short ledge, some thirty-five or forty feet into a round mirror pool . . . a charming little poem of wildness."

Today that poem can still be found, flowing from the base of Mt. Wilson into Eaton Canyon. Although it is a favored destination for many day hikers walking into this quarter of Altadena, duplicating Muir's steps in the spring can be difficult, especially if the winter has lived up to its promise.

Such was the case in 2005. This wilderness, our backyard, had taken a beating. Trails were washed out, hillsides had crumbled, and streams were swollen beyond recognition and memory.

Stepping outside—perhaps a month too early for the docent behind the counter at the Eaton Canyon Nature Center—I stole my way up this great wash. I chose not to cross the river—it was running too deep and too fast—and contented myself with skirting its city-side bank, weaving through the rock-strewn mud flats amid sabers of yucca and clumps of white sage and buckwheat, climbing the steep banks around the poison-oak-festooned toyon, laurel sumac and oak, never far from the sometimes roaring, sometimes muted crash of the river itself, knifing its way down this arroyo.

Almost one hundred years ago, such a venture was commonplace. During the Great Hiking Era—the title lent by some historians to the decades from 1900 to the 1930s—thousands of day hikers took to these mountains on weekends. Perhaps the most popular trail was to Mt. Wilson. In 1911, some 40,000 people passed through Orchard Camp, a trail resort above Sierra Madre.

Fires and floods naturally played a role in diminishing the popularity of such activity, but these mountains and the city were also victims of progress. The automobile opened faster doors of escape for us, and with the completion of the Angeles Crest Highway in 1941 and the road up San Gabriel Canyon in the mid-1930s, destinations once hiked to were now driven to. And somewhere in the development that took place across this flood plain in the wake of World War II, our relationship to this wilderness was compromised.

In an essay that is as full of love for this land as it is full of sadness for the changes that swept over it, Hildegarde Flanner wrote in 1950: "If we have anything here that could be called a tradition it lies in appreciation of the earth."

Regaining that appreciation is easier than it may seem. Leave behind the freeway traffic, politics or the potholes in our roads. Here, at Eaton Canyon, the oaks have already taken on two-toned shading as the new growth leafs out from the older, more lustrous foliage. Scrub jays flash blue from the branches of a sycamore tree. The mud at my feet holds the dried, clawed paw print of a raccoon, and up ahead, by the Eaton Canyon bridge, a landslide has wiped out the trail to Henninger Flats. It promises to be closed for at least another year.

Angelenos have always been ambivalent about indigenous pleasures. We briefly dream about the old while reaching out for the new. We build homes on the mountains we love and design them more as confrontations than complements. Green lawns become the aesthetic standard in a climate more suited for chaparral.

Perhaps deeper, though, at the heart of our ambivalence is our own wandering psyche, a reluctance to accept the fact that we might just have roots in this soil. If our history has taught us anything, it is that change is everything and that permanence is an illusion. To believe in anything else is to set us up for loss.

So we choose to live on the surface, and memory is lost in the velocity of our lives. As Carey McWilliams said more than fifty years ago, the only reality today is acceleration—a comment more true than ever before. And all the more reason to take to the hills and appreciate what this place has to give us.

On this late winter day in Eaton Canyon, the clouds in the sky are fresh from Constable's palette, and high overhead, the pines of Henninger Flats are silhouetted against the sky. Sure, underfoot are occasional cigarette butts, plastic bags, graffiti, but they don't steal from the pleasures of being here. The thatched palm trees, the lost shoe, the Gatorade empty are reminders of what lies just over the lip of that high embankment.

Visiting these mountains is a means by which we can understand who we are. Historians, especially of Los Angeles, often puzzle the intersection of imagination and identity. Coming to this land today, to the brutal topography of these mountains as they rise above the pell-mell breadth of the city, we add a new dimension to our identity, a dimension that has always been there but that we have denied, overlooked and disputed to our own loss.

Thomas Curwen

Twenty-four Hours in the Life of a California Oak

At the Cosumnes River Preserve, nightfall on a cloudless spring evening does not hurry. Wings flash across the sky, and frogs, emboldened by the fading light, take up singing as birds fall silent. Just above the horizon, a sliver of the moon emerges in the airbrushed light. Only Venus is more bright.

Back in the city, the first episode of *CSI* is about to air. Here, earth and grass are still warm, pungent from a long afternoon beneath an oak tree in the California Delta, at the confluence of the Mokelumne and Cosumnes rivers, 60 miles northeast of San Francisco. The Central Valley's last wild river, the Cosumnes originates in Eldorado National Forest in the High Sierra at 7,600 feet. It draws from a basin of 1,200 square miles and funnels down granite slopes into wooded foothills before sliding into this flatland.

Here, cottonwoods, willows, ash and oaks line its banks in a thick, hummocky profusion. California wild grape, poison oak and California blackberry intertwine in the lush understory. Beyond the river, cultivated fields, protected by levees, give way to rolling hills of dried ryegrass that spread like ocean swells around this solitary oak. A mile to the west, Interstate 5 roars with a low white noise, and a distant freight train begins its labored crescendo.

Nature's beauties are often small and patient and unnoticed. Even the most dramatic, like birth and death, are unremarkable because they take place without expectation. Wildlife is, as poet Gary Snyder reminds us, "often simply a call, a cough in the dark, a shadow in the shrubs."

A shooting star burns through the eastern sky, busy with planes and bright with the glow from Galt, an ag town of nearly 20,000.

Once an acorn—a thimble-sized nut revered by Native Californians—buried and forgotten by a squirrel or a jay, this tree grew in a world and a place we have no record of, certainly before the Gold Rush, perhaps before the arrival of the Span-ish. But an understanding of this oak begins with an appreciation of a scale of time that is unimaginable. Paleobotanists tell us that the first plants began to form nearly 375 million years ago and that in these leaves are the traces of a world still largely submerged—of giant horsetails, club mosses and ferns just starting their prehistoric climb toward the sun. Fossils of the first oak trees have been dated to nearly 45 million years ago, 40 million years before the arrival of apelike humans in Africa.

The ground slopes slightly away from the trunk, evidence of its slow growth. The rustle of the leaves rises and falls in distinct cadences as if the oak were being played by the wind, nuance modulated by the velocity of each gust. In the distance, the limbs of two trees rub one another. A great horned owl calls from across the field, then suddenly alights overhead—*who-who-who-who who-who*. Somewhere in these fields tonight a mouse or a vole will die in its talons.

There are twenty species of oaks in California, nine trees, eleven shrubs. Five trees, including this valley oak, are deciduous. These oaks once flourished along riv-ers in the Central Valley, where their roots found water no more than thirty or forty feet beneath the surface. Yet today, it and other species are threatened. Vintners ax them for more acreage, ranchers blast them for more grazing land, developers bull-doze them for more homes.

This tree has been spared. It stands nearly eighty feet tall, its trunk twelve feet around, its branches arcing out in a tangle of wood and in clusters of leaves that near-ly touch the ground. A blaze, its meaning long forgotten, scars the furrowed trunk. The ranchers who owned this property before selling it to the Nature Conservancy held barbecues here, and a former secretary of the Interior once stood at this spot.

The stars of the Big Dipper shine though the swaying canopy. Then, in an in-stant, they fade.

"Only that day dawns to which we are awake," writes Thoreau, and the awaken-ing begins with the birds, whose polyphonies quickly stake out territories lost during the night.

As light creeps into the sky, colors creep into the clouds, which break up and fracture into blues and reds and yellows. A scrub-jay squawks out of sight. Flashes of white—swallows, from the look of their tails—jet out toward the river and bank over the field.

When the sun tops a forest of oak and ash to the east, its rays turn this tree into a mosaic of light and shadow. Its branches look like tributaries, its leaves like a jigsaw puzzle. Overhead in the canopy, a bird with a soft green breast and dark wings hangs upside down, working its way through the pieces.

A house wren has made its nest in a hollowed-out limb. The chicks are hidden, but their hoarse, crackling clamor is clear. The wren jumps from branch to branch—a cricket in its mouth—before diving into the hole and hopping out as fast.

The ecosystem of an oak is one of the most varied and complex in the West. More than three hundred species of birds, mammals, reptiles and amphibians depend on these surrounding woodlands for their survival. Their names are buried in the pages of a field guide. An insect, perhaps a mayfly, a damselfly or a winged ant, lands on a nearby leaf. So much of the natural world is a mystery.

When God gave man providence over Eden, we are told, man was charged with the responsibility of naming everything he saw. The task was not a capricious one. Man in his grace knew a sparrow to be a sparrow, a fox a fox, an oak an oak. After the Fall, he lost that knowledge. After the Fall, he was separated from the world that surrounded him and ever since has tried to bridge that gap.

"The physical landscape," Barry Lopez writes, "is baffling in its ability to transcend whatever we would make of it. . . . The mind, full of curiosity and analysis, disassembles a landscape and then reassembles the pieces . . . trying to find its place within the land, to discover a way to dispel its own sense of estrangement."

When climbers ascend a face, when surfers ride a wave or rafters follow a river, the intent is the same. Beyond the thrill, the danger, the promise of success is an urge to connect with a wildness greater than and divorced from who we are.

By 10 a.m., outside the ring of this tree, red-winged blackbirds and meadowlarks flit among the cattails and reeds growing by the slough. The wind, drawn in from the Pacific by the rising valley heat, has kept the mosquitoes away. Ticks line the long stems of grass along well-trod paths, waiting to attach themselves to warm-blooded passersby.

By 11 a.m., only the house wren is active. This slow exposure to the day—to the changing light, the pace of the sun, the changing shadows—reveals black owl pellets, cast-up remnants of fur and bone that look like coyote scat, fallen in the grass that grows along the perimeter of the tree. Mistletoe hangs raggedly from the lower limbs. Wasp galls protrude from branches like forgotten Christmas ornaments.

From afar, this oak is nothing but shadow. Up close, its leaves are among the most distinctive in nature. Their lobed design has given the tree its name, Quercus lobata. One naturalist suggests that this particular shape is best suited for hot summer temperatures, that it allows not only for maximum evaporation of water—thus cooling the tree—but also that it lets more light pass through the canopy for the leaves beneath.

More than ten years ago, Bill McKibben argued that the knowledge gained in the Information Age was mostly specious. In *The Age of Missing Information*, he contrasted television with nature, mediated experience with authentic experience. "You have to listen harder to the natural world so you can separate out the primal song from the songs of our civilization and from our static," he wrote.

What is the primal song, and what is our static? A buyers' guide for an outdoors magazine recently recommended a list of seasonal supplies: sunglasses ($99), a fitness watch ($369), a digital camera ($999), binoculars ($899), a backpack ($200), shoes ($225), a tent ($285), a sleeping bag ($300), a camp stove ($80), a jacket ($119), running shoes ($110), a bike ($2,380), a kayak ($999), a sports rack ($349) and luggage ($175).

Inherent in each item is a tacit commandment to act, to move, to do. We are not often invited to be still. We speak with reverence of Thoreau's famous summer morning—"I sat in my sunny doorway from sunrise till noon, rapt in reverie. . . ." Then we pick up the trail again to some new urgency, a pressing destination. To what extent have we subjugated need to desire?

By 1 p.m., hot sunlight lances through the branches of the tree, whose shadow is slightly dappled and unmoved by the breeze. This tree is healthy. But oaks can die suddenly: one summer providing shade and the next lying split in half, dead at the core. Such a fate may await this tree, and then the field would be empty but for the snag, a decaying relic releasing its long history into the soil.

Why do we seek the outdoors? E.O. Wilson explains it with the word "biophilia": a love of nature, a genetic predisposition for wildness that goes beyond its beauty or its implicit challenge. Wilson believes that the preservation of the world lies in understanding and appreciating the wonder and awe that nature arouses.

Perhaps our avidity for nature today is a measure of our distance from it. Is it any wonder that the Romantic Movement—the tradition of such nature writers as Wordsworth and Coleridge—arose at the start of the Industrial Revolution when the splendors of their world were fast being eclipsed by the press of cities and modernity?

We grasp more anxiously for what seems out of reach, as if we need to compensate for what's missing. It's ironic, then, that we further that distance by searching for the best or doing the most and deprive ourselves of lessons that have long sustained us.

As the heat of the day peaks and wanes, the sun sneaks its rays beneath the canopy and brightens the limbs and branches of the tree. In the twilight, the lichen on the bark is surprisingly green. Twenty-four hours are nearly over. Soon the sun will set, and the world will glow, lavender spilling across the sky. And the tree itself slows, its own photosynthetic metabolism ebbing in the fading light, where somewhere an owl prepares to hunt.

"Circus Liqour"

Kevin Starr

LANDSCAPE ELECTRIC: A PROGRAM THAT RENEWS THE CITY'S URBAN SPIRIT BY RELIGHTING PHILIP MARLOWE'S NEON L.A.

Urban renewal can sometimes be an expensive proposition: tearing down entire districts, constructing vast public works, cutting through neighborhoods with freeways and boulevards. Urban renewal can sometimes function as moral renewal by tapping into better identities, energized by the best imperatives of culture and religion. Sometimes, urban renewal can be as simple as the relighting of a neon sign on Wilshire, Hollywood or Sunset Boulevard, lights that recover the past and point to an equally bright urban future.

Neon! Remnants of a lost Los Angeles, city of the mind, remembered and yearned for, the neon lights of L.A.—celestial fires of another sort, green, gold, ruby red, electric blue—guide us down the Wilshire corridor, up through Hollywood and out along Sunset Boulevard west. If Paris is the City of Lights, L.A. is the City of Neon, possessed of a comparable (yet antithetical) beauty and capable as well, like all great cities, of giving rise in the magic of the night to hungers of body, mind and spirit.

"The lights were wonderful," noted detective Philip Marlowe, driving through the city in Raymond Chandler's *The Little Sister* (1949). "There ought to be a monument to the man who invented neon lights fifteen stories high, solid marble. There's a boy who really made something out of nothing."

Something out of nothing? Is that not a good description of a town that, in the 1920s and 1930s, boomed and boosted itself into an important U.S. city? One of those boomers and boosters, Packard dealer Earle C. Anthony, visiting Paris in 1922, beheld a new kind of electric sign, devised by Georges Claude, who owned the company Claude Neon. The company made a glass tube filled with argon gas that, when an electric current passed through it, glowed with colors, sassy and bright. Like George Gershwin's "Rhapsody in Blue" (1924), neon announced the 1920s as a decade enamored of urban sophistication. Before he returned home, Anthony commissioned three orange and blue neon signs saying "Packard," one of which he installed in 1923 atop his dealership.

Over the next two decades, until 1942, Wilshire Boulevard, together with the boulevards of Hollywood, thrust Los Angeles into a golden age of neon. Few aspects of the city were more expressive of the improbable, even arcane nature of L.A. than these pathways of light, which, like the city itself, took simple materials and made of them a visual landscape and language of dreams.

Driving down these neon corridors by night, writers such as James M. Cain, Horace McCoy, John O'Hara, F. Scott Fitzgerald, Nathanael West, William Faulkner, Christopher Isherwood, Budd Schulberg and Raymond Chandler, epic poet of the city, felt themselves in the presence, as Fitzgerald put it, of a vast and meretricious beauty: a city in the borderlands of fact and fantasy, dream and desire, corruption and innocence. For Chandler especially, the neon-lit hotels, apartment houses, stores, bars, restaurants and theaters offered by night a landscape electric with subliminal power.

Cuban-born Adolfo V. Nodal, today general manager of the city's Cultural Affairs Department, felt the power of these neon signs in a direct and personal way. Perhaps it was because pre-Castro Havana was also a city of neon light, or perhaps it was because Nodal, a Chandler fan, had just finished *The Little Sister*, with its brief but effective testimony to the power of neon. In any event, Nodal devoted himself to relighting the neon signs surrounding MacArthur Park. It turned out to be the first step of a decade-plus program called LUMENS, an acronym for Living Urban Museum of Electric and Neon Signs but also a play on the Latin word for light. At the relatively minor cost of about $ 400,000, LUMENS has relit dozens of neon signs along what is today called the Historic Wilshire Neon Corridor. The program is currently taking aim at forty-three neon signs in the Historic Hollywood Neon District.

In February 1942, after an air-raid scare, Mayor Fletcher Bowron ordered the neon lights of L.A. turned off, lest they guide Japanese planes or offshore submarines (Goleta, near Santa Barbara, had just been shelled) to their targets. Already, many neon signs had gone dim in the Depression, casualties of hard times. Thus, starting in the mid-1980s with the MacArthur Park Project, when electrical contractor Ray Neal, owner of Sun Valley-based Standard Electrical Services, took his electricians atop roofs of MacArthur Park and Wilshire, they encountered signs that had been dim for as long as sixty years. The oldest sign to be restored, the animated bowler announcing Jensen's Recreation Center in Echo Park (technically not neon but incandescent lamp in its technology), dated from 1919.

Miraculously—and here also is a powerful symbol for urban renewal—most of the neon signs were in pretty good structural shape after more than a half century on the skyline. Some of them still had vestiges of their original gas. Most needed little structural repair and could be brought back to light within two weeks, with the installation of new tubes, wiring and transformers. Electricians discovered that more than seven hundred sockets of the nearly eighty-year-old Jensen's Recreation Center sign were in working order.

Elected officials were quick to grasp the implications of Nodal's proposal to re-light the city. LUMENS used existing resources, for one thing; it was simple and easy to understand; it recovered a valuable aspect of the Los Angeles heritage; and, like neon always will, it bespoke the magic of the city. Mayor Richard Riordan, then running for reelection, and City Council members Nate Holden, Jackie Goldberg, Mike Hernandez and John Ferraro, in whose districts could be found the bulk of surviving neon, were early backers of LUMENS, as was John Molloy of the Community Redevelopment Agency. In June 1996, these officials and others gathered for a ceremony in which Riordan, to commemorate the completion of the first phase of the project, flipped a switch that illuminated twenty-five restored neon signs along the Wilshire corridor. Then on to Hollywood, where forty-three surviving, relight-able neon signs had been located.

Nodal and his colleagues in the Cultural Affairs Department must be credited for one of the most imaginative and cost-effective redevelopment schemes in Los Angeles history. The LUMENS project has literally relit history and has brought forward to present-day L.A. the mood and mystery of the city in its Chandler years. The city also supports the Museum of Neon Art, which preserves signs and displays original electronic art. The museum received a grant from the city that helped it re-locate downtown, to the neighborhood where Anthony's Packard sign convoked car culture's brash blend of consumerism and high style. One need only to drive the out-er portions of Sunset Boulevard, a pathway of garish light leading to the wine-dark sea, to realize that contemporary neon is alive and well in L.A. The re-illuminated signs of the LUMENS project and the Museum of Neon Art, however, supplement the largely Hollywood and motion-picture-oriented neon of the late 1990s with the more subdued visual signatures of an earlier, literature-dominated era.

These relit signs, after all, are the very signs that guided Marlowe through the city on a thousand lonely nights. Wilshire Ebell, Ancelle, Gaylord, Hollywood Roos-evelt, Hollywood Wilcox, Max Factor, Egyptian, Pantages, Musso & Frank, Hotel Knickerbocker, Taft Building: These are the signs that captivated Chandler as the perfect symbol of Los Angeles as a city of illusion struggling up from the shadow-lands of its submerged psychic life to the rooftop glitz and glamour of neon. Even today, the Newbury School of Beauty sign on Hollywood Boulevard bespeaks the dreams of glamour that were then bringing, and still continue to bring, generations of young women to the city, hoping for success in the movies.

El Royale and Ravenswood signs on Rossmore, Vivian apartments on North Bronson, Castle Argyle on South Westlake, De Mille Manor on Argyle—all still evoke the domestic dramas, the private ordeals and triumphs that transpired on these premises in the Chandler era.

A platinum blond lights a cigarette by the nighttime window. She stares out across the darkened city at the other neon lights. Pinching a fleck of tobacco from her tongue with manicured nails, she inhales once again. Arching her pencil-thin eyebrows, she hears the knock at the door, the ring of the telephone. Her name is Carole, Norma, Bette, Joan, Barbara—whatever. Her real name is Los Angeles. She is at once a survivor and a doomed dame. She is sexy, brassy, vibrant, a daughter of the Midwest, half-frightened yet thrilled with what she has become here on the coast. She is enamored of the vast and improbable pageant—and the loneliness—of her life.

The neon sign atop her apartment building casts its opalescent light, the colors of the 1930s—ruby red, electric blue, lime green—across her made-up face. She waits in the darkness amid the neon for the future she is determined to make happen. Let it come now! Let the knock on the door, the ring of the telephone, be the beginning of what she had come here for in the first place, a new life. She'll take it all and be glad of it: the big dreams, the kisses, the glory, the laughs, the tears, the bad falls—the long goodbyes.

Meghan Daum

CLICHE AND CATACLYSM

Whenever California burns or shakes or collapses in mudslides, a cavalcade of familiar noir-isms comes along for the ride. Social critics wax nihilistic about impermanence as a permanent state of mind. Inevitably, Joan Didion quotes blow in like the Santa Anas themselves, offering up heavy doses of the line about the winds forcing an acceptance of "a deeply mechanistic view of human behavior." Inevitably, references will be made to Nathaniel West's *The Day of the Locust*, to Raymond Chandler's *Red Wind*, even to Steely Dan lyrics.

This hip mix of dread and sang-froid, especially when it comes to natural disasters, is crucial to our regional literary and cinematic identity. In hard times, New Englanders may have their flinty stoicism, Southerners their gothic rhapsody and Midwesterners their sandbags. But when it comes to the way we respond to apocalyptic tragedy, citizens of the Golden State seem marked by a grim nonchalance. As bad as things get, we never entirely let go of the idea that a Californian watches his house burn down while standing in his driveway in a pair of Ray-Bans, drinking gin and humming a Doors song.

Such caliginous images are not just a mythology we impart to the outside world, they're integral to the clichés that remind us why we live here. In the same way that New York City dwellers wear the hassles of their daily lives as a badge of honor, Californians like to view their proximity to impending disaster as a direct reflection of their toughness; evidence that they're more interesting, more glamorous than everyone else—and the closer they live to the precarious edge, the more quintessentially Californian they are.

Of course, this form of interestingness comes at a price, most notably the price of real estate. And the fact that the most at-risk property in the region is also the most expensive makes our apocalypse narratives that much more enticing. "There were no streetlights . . . that was one of the attractions," writes T. Coraghessan Boyle in *The Tortilla Curtain*, a novel in which the craggy topography of canyon life obscures the view of unpleasant social realities (though not for long). "The rural feel, the sense that you were somehow separated from the city and wedded to the mountains . . . there were even stars, a cluster here and there fighting through the wash of light pollution."

This "rural feel," authentic enough to include wild animals and hemp sandals yet not so extreme as to involve excessively long airport commutes, is, to many people, the whole point of living in California. The West Coast analog to the sprawling (and rent-controlled) Manhattan apartment with a river for a view and Thomas Pynchon for a neighbor, a house among steep banks of chaparral is what we think about when we think about making it big.

But while New Yorkers compensate for their cramped quarters and ubiquitous vermin with constant announcements about the inferiority of everywhere else, Californians defend their turf with a curious inversion of that method. We use the sure and certain knowledge of impending disaster as a dramatic device. For all the reasons to be here, the best one is that it can seem close to Eden, and for the sake of paradise, we not only accept the cataclysm on the horizon, we embrace it.

It is, of course, unlikely that everyone—make that anyone—whose homes were destroyed or threatened were able to distract themselves from the tragedy with Heideggerian thoughts about the inevitable hopelessness of existence. We may have a literature and a mythology of cool detachment, but, in real life, people are crying and falling apart and searching in vain for their pets just as they would anywhere.

And, of course, it's never just cul-de-sac McMansions and designer homes in Malibu that get in on the calamity. As the week ended, there were nearly 2,000 homes (mountain cabins and suburban ranchettes, mobile homes and landmark castles) destroyed, seventy-nine people injured and at least seven people killed, including four migrants who apparently died while crossing the border. It has been Armageddon-like, and not exactly in a way that demands a Jim Morrison soundtrack.

Didion called Los Angeles weather "the weather of catastrophe, of apocalypse." Chandler, for his part, described windy Santa Ana nights when "meek little wives feel the edge of a carving knife and study their husbands' necks." This is sexy stuff, but it's also what we use to deny our own role in the mess.

Yes, Mother Nature is mercurial, and yes, the winds that blow in from the desert have certain otherworldly qualities. But to become over-reliant on our disaster mythology, as poetic as it is, is to carry on a heedless romance with California rather than the respectful, mature relationship that ought to develop at some point in the love affair.

Didion wrote, "We tell ourselves stories in order to live." But in order to live here, we also need clichés.

This piece was written October 26, 2007 during a particularly brutal Los Angeles fire season.

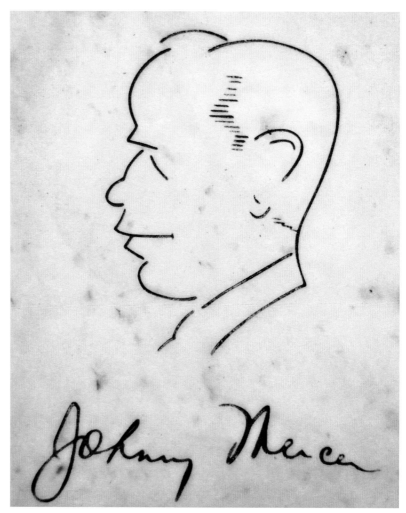

"Johnny Mercer"

Erika Schickel

When Night Was Falling

In the winter of 1975 my family made our annual trip from our home in New York to Los Angeles to visit my mother's parents. Designed by my Granddaddy in the '50s, their house was a sleek, Neutra-inspired affair perched on a Pacific Palisades hillside, offering a sweeping ocean view that an eleven-year-old couldn't have cared less about.

But the house itself was the ideal setting for a girl living in her own MGM musical—all glass doors, white floors, stylishly decorated by my Grandma Dorothy. A palm tree grew out of the living room floor and crystals splashed rainbows across the walls. I'd slide across the slick, terrazzo floors in sock feet like Gene Kelly in An American in Paris or clickety-tap on them in my Mary Janes like Fred Astaire. I could tinkle the keys on the white baby grand, or bob like a Ziegfield Girl in the sunken bathtub, surrounded by jungle fronds, lathering up with richly scented, seashell-shaped soaps. I spent hours in the swimming pool, smiling underwater like Esther Williams, and lounged in "the chatter pit," a subjacent, shag-lined den that had a TV with a remote control. I sprawled on the banquette sofa like Jeannie in her bottle, blinking my way through channels, searching for my favorite TV shows on the unfamiliar West Coast stations.

On this particular trip, my grandparents threw one of their big parties. I helped prep, buffing their colored, Lucite coffee table knickknacks, Windexing the huge, sliding glass doors, lighting and launching floating candles onto the pool. Their guests were a mix of comedy writers and tennis partners, all of whom seemed incredibly old, smoky and uninterested in me. Forgotten by the grownups, I stayed up way past my bedtime, gorging on Spanish peanuts, lulled by the drone of adult conversation. It was late in the evening when my mother found me out by the pool, woozy with Shirley Temples.

"There's someone inside I want you to meet," she said.

"Who?"

"His name is Johnny Mercer. He's an old friend. You've met him once before, but you probably won't remember him."

"Mommy . . ." I whined, not wanting to give up my warm, sleepy spot by the lava brazier.

"He wrote the lyrics for a lot of famous movie songs."

"Really, like what?"

"*Seven Brides for Seven Brothers, Breakfast at Tiffany's, Darling Lili.*"

I was suddenly wide awake. I loved all those movies, but *Darling Lili* was my current obsession. Though I had never seen the movie, I had spent that fall memorizing the soundtrack album.

Mercer was alone in my Grandaddy's study. This room was different from the others. It wasn't like a movie set, it was a real place where actual work happened. The walls were hung with photos and memorabilia from a lifetime spent writing radio, sitcoms, movies and magazines. There were awards, autographed posters and framed Playbills. Stacks of scripts surrounded his typewriter. The room was dim and had the sweet, pungent smell of pipe smoke mixed with corkboard and chlorine. Mr. Mercer, sitting on a low sofa, looked like an ordinary old man. I had half hoped he'd be wearing a top hat and tails, but he was in slacks and a sports coat. He had a kind smile and seemed tired. He greeted me warmly and asked me the usual kid questions; how old was I, how did I like school, was I having a fun trip? Then he said, "Your mother tells me you're a fan of my songs."

"Did you really write 'Darling Lili?'"

"Well, I wrote the lyrics. Do you have a favorite song?"

"'The Girl in No Man's Land.'"

"*Really?*" He seemed surprised and interested. I sensed I had an audience, something I was always on the lookout for.

"I can sing it for you if you'd like."

Mercer laughed, then looked me in the eye. "Would you? That would be lovely."

Suddenly my whole body got hot and clammy as I realized what I'd gotten myself into. I straightened up and started the first verse in a soft, wobbly voice.

They tell a story back in London town
That when you hear taps sound
Then all you soldiers have a sweetheart
Who always comes around

I knew I could sing this song better. I closed my eyes and pretended I was back in my living room in New York.

> *When night is falling*
> *She comes calling*
> *The girl in no man's land . . .*

I picked up steam and as so often happened, I became taken by the sound of my own voice. I fancied I sang it just like Julie Andrews did on the album. I opened my eyes to see a look of utter shock on Mercer's face which made me go up on the next lyric, "Doughboys weary . . . Doughboys weary . . ." I faltered and stammered. I had no clearer an idea of what the next lyric was than I did of what a doughboy was.

". . . Cold and lonely . . ." Mercer fed me the line and the rest of the song came rushing back.

I finished and Mr. Mercer applauded me. My mother draped her arm around my shoulder and I noticed that Granddaddy had slipped into the room. He stared at me from under bushy eyebrows as though as he were seeing me for the first time. I assumed these grownups were all stunned by my exquisite voice, but now, thirty years later, I think it may simply have been the incongruity of an eleven-year-old girl singing a ballad about a hooker.

Mr. Mercer thanked me and I left him. A month later I received a package of *Darling Lili* production stills and a note from him, thanking me again for my song. He died the following year. It wasn't until much later that I truly realized who I had serenaded in my grandfather's study, and how many songs Mercer had written that I love to this day. Only now can I appreciate that a child memorizing his songs may have meant a lot to a man whose life—and work—were nearly over.

The house my grandfather designed is still up on Tellem Drive. I drove out there with my eleven-year-old daughter on a whim one day and parked. There had always been a rivulet of water running down the gutter off the curb, where I would spend hours as a child launching tiny leaf boats into the downhill torrent. It was still flowing, and the sight of that current made my heart launch. I could not resist knocking on the door. The house was owned by a distinguished German film actor, and his son graciously gave me a tour. The master bath had been remodeled, but the rest of the house was just as I recalled it, though time and my own adult scale made it seem smaller and dingier. We went out the sliding glass doors to the pool—I took a picture of Franny standing by the lava brazier. She was the same age as I had been that night, and had inherited my family's love of musical theater and had a head full of Sondheim lyrics. I thought about all the people—old then and gone now—who had gathered to drink, laugh and spin their tales of young Hollywood—a place and time that has long since faded into black-and-white.

Lisa See

Have Roots, Will Travel

Many people are lured to Los Angeles because they think it has no history and they can escape their pasts and reinvent themselves. That's not me. My great-great-grandmother—a single mother with an entrepreneurial spirit—came here from Washington State to start her own business. My great-grandfather came from a small village in China and became the patriarch of Los Angeles' Chinatown. This makes me a fifth-generation Angeleno, and I'm pretty confident you won't meet many people like me. (In the interest of full disclosure, I was born in Paris, where my parents were students, but I don't count that six-week aberration.) My sons are sixth-generation Angelenos—as rare around here as snowflakes.

As a girl, I spent a lot of time with my grandparents and other relatives in our family's antiques store in Chinatown. My grandparents used to take me to a restaurant we called "the little place" to have what was then called *cha nau* (and is now more popularly known as *dim sum*). Later we'd go shopping along Spring Street: to the International Grocery for preserved turnip, fermented tofu and sesame-seed candies; to the Sam Sing Butcher Shop, with its life-size gold-leafed pig in the window; and to the Lime House for Chinese custard pie.

But visiting my grandparents was about much more than things Chinese. One block south of my family's store was El Pueblo, the city's birthplace and home to Olvera Street—a tourist destination in the guise of an "authentic" Mexican marketplace. Since 1781, El Pueblo has been a place where art, culture, politics and rabble-rousers of every stripe have congregated. But what most people don't know is that in addition to the original Yagna Indian, Spanish and Mexican settlements, Los Angeles' first Chinatown stood here; not only did the whole city ripple out from El Pueblo, but my family did as well. My great-grandparents had a store here, and my grandfather's restaurant, facing the original "Spanish plaza," was only the seventh family-style Chinese restaurant in the city. I used to think my grandmother liked to take me to El Pueblo for "Spanish" food—the "polite" name for Mexican food in those days—but now I understand that she liked to go there to remember her past.

Sometimes we'd continue to Little Tokyo, where my grandmother would buy interesting fabrics or pretty stationery. Other times we'd leave the family store and head a couple of blocks north along Broadway and then cut over to Hill Street to visit someone at the French Hospital, one of only two vestiges of what had once been a vibrant Frenchtown. (Philippe's restaurant, self-described home of the original French-dip sandwich, was just across the street from my family's store.) Much of the property along Broadway—today the main drag of Chinatown—is still owned by Italian families; that area used to be Little Italy. Today, the descendants of those pioneer families rent to immigrants from Vietnam, Cambodia, Laos and China. I sometimes wonder if this single square mile or so has more layers of people, cultures and food than any other in the country.

It seems that once my relatives got here, they just had to see, do, eat and play their ways across the city—in good times and bad. My Chinese great-grandfather loved cars and bought a new one every year, although he never learned to drive. (His sons drove him around, and he let others borrow his car to advertise their businesses.) My great-grandmother Jessie and her husband, Harvey, were itinerant workers who followed harvests and whatever other work they could get from Alaska down to the Mexican border. Jessie's diary, written from 1905 to 1937, describes how, once she moved to Los Angeles, she loved to get behind the wheel of some beat-up jalopy or other and drive hither, thither and yon to find bootleggers, go dancing or bail Harvey out of jail. (He ended up "on the nickel," living and dying homeless on Fifth Street.) All this driving—crisscrossing the city—took a long time back then, between breakdowns, dirt roads, flat tires, scarce gas stations and run-ins with the law. But this didn't stop them, nor did it stop my mother's parents after one came from Texas, the other from New York State. So I guess my desire to explore the city is genetic.

By the time I came along, in 1955, my parents lived on a "walk street"—a street reserved for pedestrians—off Hyperion Avenue between the enclaves of Silver Lake and Echo Park. Once when I was a toddler, I sped out the screen door, zipped down the walk street, made a left at Hyperion and ambled along the sidewalk until a policeman spotted me. He took me back to my mom, who was horrified and embarrassed, but to this day she remains amused and bewildered by the fact that my nature was evident at such a young age.

I still feel the need to see what's out there. Like my parents, grandparents and great-grandparents before me, I love to get in my car, roll down the windows, turn up the radio and drive. (By now you must be thinking: No wonder Los Angeles has so much traffic! No wonder it has so much smog! What about global warming? And you'd have a point, although in my defense, I drive a Prius and explore a lot on foot, too.)

My first memories are of a truly decrepit downtown tenement; now I live in lush, celebrity-studded Brentwood. In all, I've lived in more than ten different parts of the city. Along the way, I've endured fires, floods, earthquakes and landslides. I've met surfers and hippies, seen a neighborhood turn into a ghetto and encountered deer, coyotes, opossums, raccoons, every kind of rat and a mountain lion. I've crossed the city in search of the best Korean *bibimbap*, Salvadoran *pupusas* and Ethiopian food I eat with my fingers. I'm old enough to remember the Watts riot, and my sons remember what happened after the Rodney King verdict.

Here's the thing: all this diversity comes at a price, and it hasn't always been a black-and-white, rich-and-poor or north-and-south-of-the-border issue. Los Angeles' first race riot occurred in Chinatown in 1871, when nineteen Chinese men and boys were stabbed, hanged or shot to death. In 1945, on the day my aunt Sissee got married, my great-great-uncle was driving to church on the recently completed freeway. The kids got rowdy in the back seat, and one of my cousins (so many times removed) fell out of the car. It was fortunate he only broke his arm—the French Hospital wouldn't treat him because he was Chinese. In 1957, when my great-grandfather died, the City Council honored him as a Los Angeles pioneer, but one cemetery refused to bury him because he was Chinese. My parents were only the second mixed-race couple in my family to marry legally in this country; California law banned marriage between Chinese and Caucasians until 1948. And that's just one family's story. I like to think we can learn from the past, but as the film *Crash* illustrated, we're constantly bumping into each other, and on any given day anything can happen in the City of Angels.

I'm a city commissioner now and serve on the El Pueblo de Los Angeles Historical Monument Authority, which twice a month brings me back to my family's and my city's roots. Lately, after commission meetings, I've been walking to the block where my family had their store when I was growing up. Philippe's is still in business, and the double-dipped pork sandwich there is still the best. But these days I feel compelled to wend my way around the world by circling that single block, where I

HAVE ROOTS,
WILL TRAVEL

have the choice of takeout from Mexican, Filipino, Peruvian, Thai, Chinese or Texas barbecue restaurants. Then I get in my car and head home.

Sometimes I take the freeway, but often I head west on Sunset Boulevard to travel through time, passing old neighborhoods with houses clinging to hillsides and bungalows swathed in Cecile Brunner roses, and then threading through the run-down decadence of Hollywood, with its prostitutes and by-the-hour motels, the fading hipness of the Sunset Strip and Beverly Hills, with its mansions and broad green lawns. Often, I don't see Los Angeles as it is—so much of it new, so much of it still trying to define itself—but as it was. I see the city of my childhood, the lingering echoes of my family and a history that's deep, complex and not always wonderful. It's a city beautiful, melancholy and triumphant, and it's my home.

T. Jefferson Parker

THE MIRACLE MILES

Last trout season, two writer friends of mine flew into Los Angeles to fly-fish the Eastern Sierra. The guy from Cheyenne, Wyoming, wore a big black Stetson. The one from Brooklyn wore red sneakers. They both dragged gigantic rolling duffels weighted with fly-fishing gear. They were happy to be in California and serious about catching fish. They expected me to show them the ropes.

Showing these accomplished anglers the ropes was an amusing notion: Chuck Box—"C.J."—is a former fishing guide from Cheyenne, and Brian Wiprud, our Brooklynite, was just back from fly-fishing in the jungles of Brazil. Or was it the mountains of Kenya? Between them, they had fly-fished for fifty years. I had scratched out ten, maybe. It didn't matter to these men: They wanted Sierra trout, and they wanted them now. I was elected to deliver. The heat was on.

Luckily, I had help. Our friend Ken Wilson, a well-known L.A. book publicist, volunteered to co-chair the event, so Ken and I picked up C.J. and Brian at the airport terminal and headed out.

We're in my Ford, James McMurtry on CD and mountains of gear in the back. We spend the first half-hour catching up on things—our families, our book deals, our ailments and remedies—but four anglers headed for the water can only talk about things not fish for about 40 minutes, tops. By the time we hit U.S. 395, Chuck is telling us about a large brown trout he recently took from a Wyoming pond on a mouse imitation.

"The mouse had wobbling eyes, and I think they helped attract that brown," he says with apparent sincerity.

"That's ridiculous," Brian says.

Chuck produces the mouse from a shirt pocket and passes it around. It's a cute little thing with a leather tail, a hook hidden in its belly fur, and sure enough, the eyes really do wobble. Fly-fishers learn early that verisimilitude doesn't mean squat to fish—except when it means everything.

Brian doubtfully examines the mouse. He shakes it so the eyes move. "I made a mouse out of brown shag carpet once."

"Catch anything with it?" Chuck asks.

"Naw. Fell apart."

"It looked more like a toupee than a mouse," Ken says.

Brian has dug out one of his many fly boxes to show us some of the flies he tied for this trip.

A well-appointed fly box is a thing of minor beauty. There are platoons of caddisflies, sizes 12 to 18, in olive and gray and tan. There are legions of blue-winged olive mayfly dressings, and pale morning mayfly duns, and Royal Wulffs with their showy flashes of red.

"But where are the streamers?" Chuck asks.

"Right here."

Brian is, among other things, our streamer guy. He sets down the first box and finds another, larger one. He opens it, and they pass it around. From the corner of my eye, I see olive and black and brown feathers wafting in the A/C breeze.

I can't really look at Brian's craft work because I'm driving. And I'm aware that we're barely past Adelanto. CHP is thick in here, but I haven't fished a river since November. I can't remember what kind of pie I ate at Thanksgiving all those five months ago, but I can tell you exactly where I was standing (first curve of Upper Owens at the monument) when I caught my last fish of the year (a small rainbow) and what I caught it on (No. 18 zebra midge). I turn up the McMurtry and goose the cruise control a little higher over the speed limit.

The miles become shorter, almost friendly.

Four Corners.

Red Mountain.

Randsburg. Ken wants to know if anyone wants to stop to see the old saloons and jail and mining equipment. He has a deep appreciation for California history.

I join the surly chorus of boos and stomp on the gas.

We make Hot Creek by late afternoon. In a fecund stretch, we stealthily approach trout holding in the shallow clear water. These fish are the stuff of legend—often enormous, popular with the masses, extremely difficult to fool. Anglers from all over the world go slack-jawed when they see these things for the first time.

They're feeding in their respective lanes, nosing into the current for changes of direction, then sliding back into their slots. Trout, of course, are territorial, and the biggest ones get the best lies. The biggest one looks to be twenty-six inches long, and I say so.

"It's only twenty-four," Brian says. "The water is magnifying it."

"I can't believe the size of that thing," says Chuck, who is no stranger to the big fish of Wyoming's North Platte. "Brian, if you don't catch it, I'm going to."

Brian sidles downstream and ties on a 4X leader, which is quite large for this clear smooth water, but anything finer would be snapped off by such large fish.

The trout is feeding up in the water column, not down low, not at the surface. Brian ties on a wet fly; it sinks a little and imitates an aquatic insect struggling toward the surface to use its wings for the first time. He makes a slow, hunched-down approach from behind.

He'll get only one cast, and it will have to be perfect. With a fish that has seen as many flies as this one, it's first cast or never. One shot. He'll have to figure in the breeze and get that fly way upstream of the trout, then mend the line away from the fish so he doesn't scare it off.

All of which he does perfectly. The wet fly swings into the big rainbow's lane twenty feet upstream. The fish locks onto it early. Target acquired. You can tell by its tiny angle of adjustment. The fish sways, waiting. Four hearts pause; four nervous systems go code blue. The huge trout bullets forward with immeasurable velocity, aimed directly at the fly. Then, as if hitting some invisible wall, it veers past the fly and disappears.

Why?

Did the hook glimmer in the sunlight?

Did the tippet show in the clear water?

Did the wet fly look not quite natural?

Well, we'll never know. Whatever it was, it's part of the reason this fish is 24 inches long.

In the silence that follows, my emotions shift like gears: hope, hope dashed, beauty appreciated, beauty lost, riches glimpsed, emptiness. I look up at the Sierra. They do not register our plight. I join the cussing.

Now this run of Hot Creek is vacant, not a fish to be seen. A spooked king is a spooked kingdom. And there are truckloads of anglers pulling up for their shot at these crafty monsters.

The next day, we fish Rock Creek (west of Tom's Place) as a way to run up some numbers and see some beautiful country. Rock Creek is full of brook trout, which of the four main strains of trout—brown, rainbow, cutthroat, brook—are generally regarded as the easiest to catch.

They are also, for my money, the most beautiful. And I love the reckless abandon with which they attack flies. They're notoriously aggressive, and sure enough, they're lining up to hit our flies.

Fishing a pool, Ken snatches up twelve in about five minutes without moving from his spot. Chuck seems to be hooked up on every cast. Brian catches some then disappears upstream. I find a pod of brook trout that can't resist my pale morning dun mayfly. My kind of fish: pretty and dumb.

I find Brian around the bend, pulling fish out of a small Sierra lake so clear that the upside-down reflections of the mountains on its surface are nearly as precise and pristine as the mountains themselves.

"We don't have this in Brooklyn," he says.

By day's end we've caught and released 155 trout among us. We guess that our 155 fish would weigh about the same as the twenty-four-inch heartbreaker in Hot Creek the day before, but this does not dim our spirits.

We agree to try the big Hot Creek rainbow again tomorrow.

Trekking back to the truck, we're all yapping away about the fish, then about Jim Harrison's new book, then more about the fish, then about Chuck seeing McMurtry play in Austin. It's one of those four-way conversations that has no true north but lots of enthusiasm. We stop at the trail crest to take pictures. The view is magnificent.

Up the trail come hikers. They're smothered by backpacks, leaning forward against the grade, staffs tapping, boots crunching up dust on the trail. They're setting a good pace, trying to beat the sunset to the lake. I can hear their shortened breathing. They glance and nod at us as we move aside to let them pass.

I take another picture. My heart is full, and my casting shoulder is sore.

I feel sorry for people who don't fish.

Carolyn Kellogg

Death Valley

In 1913, when the temperature reached 134 degrees, Death Valley broke all previous records and became the hottest place on earth. (Although a scorching 136 was later reached in the Sahara, Death Valley remains at number two). Death Valley is so hot and so dry that water is sucked from the ground, leaving a parched, cracked salt flat forty miles long and five miles wide. Some desert plant roots stretch fifty feet down to reach the water they need. As America's hottest, driest place, it is incredibly inhospitable to life.

Which makes the thirty-five years of solo ballerina performances that took place on its edge, in Death Valley Junction, all the more remarkable.

Marta Becket, on hiatus from dancing in New York, was driving the California desert with her husband when their car broke down. She wandered off during the repairs, coming across a boarded-up adobe hall.

Becket peered in and saw a slant of light, dust. And in that instant, she was struck with a kind of love. "As if I was looking at the other half of myself," she would later repeat, "like I was looking in a mirror."

It was 1967, when dropping out was all the rage, and before the day was through the forty-three-year-old Becket and her husband decided to leave New York behind. They would rent the hall and stay in Death Valley Junction, a town with a population smaller than the companies of the Broadway shows Becket used to perform in.

The town's adobe buildings had been constructed by Borax in the early 1920s for its staff. Some say the soap maker, which was mining in Death Valley, built the picturesque square only after Zane Grey published an article excoriating the company for its atrocious desert working conditions. By 1928, Borax left it all behind in favor of kinder environs.

Forty years later, Becket got the hall into shape and opened it with a grand new name: the Amargosa Opera House.

Three nights a week, Becket pulled on her tights, curved her feet into toe shoes, and took the stage. She performed for whomever would come, even if the audience was small. Even if they didn't know much about ballet. Even when there wasn't anyone there—which, admittedly, happened a lot.

Marta Becket's story is, in part, a case of art for art's sake. Her New York dance career was coming to a close, and she found a way to keep performing, on her own terms, purely for the dance.

Sort of.

Because what she felt when she danced to no one at all was not complete satisfaction. Although she had chosen to live in one of the most desolate places on earth, she still wanted to be seen. Performing to an empty room was not enough: Marta Becket needed the gaze of an audience.

So as the ceaseless winter winds blew and the summer brought weeks of hundred-degree days and then the gray winter came around again, Marta Becket, between dances, conjured an audience. For four years, she imagined eyes upon her—with a paintbrush in her hand.

She painted a roomful of spectators: balconies and private boxes, ladies and knights and nuns, bullfighters and a king and queen. She went from floor to ceiling, and then she painted the ceiling, too. She used lush reds and golds, and if her style was a bit awkward, it made the old meeting room feel like the opera house she imagined. She would never perform to an empty room again.

And while she couldn't have known it when she began, her paintings ensured that the room would fill with people, real live warm-bodied people. Not for the art so much as for the inspiration of it all: imagining a place of beauty in that desert corner, creating what she needed to sustain her, performing without fail. Although her husband left in the early '80s, another man stepped to her side. Together they ran a hotel in another of the old adobe structures, where Becket's paintings guarantee there was always someone hanging out in the lobby. Five hours from Los Angeles, two hours from Las Vegas, Death Valley Junction and the Amargosa Opera House have welcomed a steady stream of acolytes for decades. Even today, dressed in blue velvet, eighty-five-year-old Marta Becket takes the stage regularly to tell her story.

Like so many of us, Marta Becket came here from somewhere else, deciding that California presented a chance for rejuvenation and an artistic life. Others found a more gentle state; Becket chose an isolated, abandoned district on the edge of the nation's most brutal desert. With her astonishing determination and vision, she proved that an individual artist can follow her own path and get exactly the fame she deserves—even when that means exposing her need for an audience that always smiles.

"Yurok Canoe on Trinity River"

Tony Platt

SECOND HOME, FIRST HOME

"The tectonic layers of our lives rest so tightly one on top of the other that we always come up against earlier events in later ones, not as matter that has been fully formed and pushed aside, but absolutely present and alive."
—Bernhard Schlink, *The Reader*, 1995

"History is an argument about the past, as well as the record of it, and its terms are forever changing. . . ."
—Raphael Samuel, *Theatres of Memory*, 1994

Peel back layers of a landscape and you'll unearth many histories. Which ones we remember are a matter of choice, morality, and clout.

I arrived in Berkeley in 1963, a twenty-one year old immigrant from the provinces of northern England. I was here for graduate school, temporarily I thought, ready to climb the first rung into the meritocracy, and then return to the homeland. But the magnetism of the student movement and seduction of an expanding academic job market in the United States quickly changed my mind. By 1968, after two years on a fellowship in Chicago, I was back at Berkeley as a junior professor, married with two kids, a mortgage, and an occasional fantasy about a getaway place on the northwest coast.

It wasn't until the late 1970s, now divorced, that I found a cabin by the ocean that I and my girlfriend could afford, and even then we had to recruit another couple to split the costs. In 1978, we paid $25,000 for a small, two-bedroom retreat—about 700 square feet—in Big Lagoon, Humboldt County. The previous owner had bought the place four years earlier for $2,000, plus $50 for some appliances, from a local Native American family. Today, even with a shaky housing market, the cabin has increased its value about fifty-fold in the last thirty-five years.

With its intimate mingling of ocean, lagoon, and forest, Big Lagoon is a unique habitat. A mixed-use, commerce-free village, bounded by the Pacific Ocean on its west and Highway 101 to its east, its northern boundary ends with a three-mile lagoon, part of California's state park system. To its south, buffered by a subdivision along the cliffs, is Patrick's Point State Park. Big Lagoon itself includes a county and state park, a public elementary school, the thirty-eight acre Big Lagoon Indian Rancheria on the southern shore of the lagoon, and a sixty-acre private recreational community in Big Lagoon's southwest corner, where I co-own one of seventy-six cabins.

In addition to its few year-round residents, many visitors come to Big Lagoon for swimming and boating in the lagoon, to walk a long beach that rims the fierce ocean, and to camp in a scenic copse. The land that was home to many native settlements for at least forty generations and a site of historical significance is unprotected and unmarked. Unknowingly, many day-trippers park their cars on top of O-pyúweg, or Where They Dance, once a large Yurok town.

I've been coming to Big Lagoon for more than thirty years, first with my children, and then their children. Even on a calm night, in our cabin some two hundred yards from the Pacific you can hear the kettledrum booming of waves hitting the shore. At the coast, a barrier beach runs for about three miles north of our cabin until you reach a place where Big Lagoon, fattened by streams and rain, occasionally leaks into the Pacific and where the ocean at extreme high tide pours its brackish waves into the lagoon. For most of the year, however, these two extraordinarily different bodies of water coexist a stone's throw apart. If you stand exactly in the middle of the beach, one ear is deafened by the ocean's roar, while the other can hear the whoosh of brown pelicans as they alight clumsily on the placid lagoon. And this détente has lasted perhaps a millennium, as we know from tales passed on by the Yurok.

It's three hundred miles from our house in Berkeley to our second home, now co-owned by my wife Cecilia and myself, and two other couples—close enough to make it there by car in six hours, but far enough away to make me feel as though I'm getting away from it all. Once you get beyond Santa Rosa and the sprawling exurbia of the Bay Area, Highway 101 winds through Sonoma's overdeveloped wine country and corporate farmland until you reach Humboldt's largest and once prosperous city, Eureka.

During the 1950s, about one of every two working people in the county was involved in lumber production, and families were better off than most folks in the country. But by the 1960s, as the housing boom receded, Eureka began its steep descent to hard times. Now it's a hardscrabble place, with one out of five people living below the poverty line, and many others just hanging on. And like the rest of the county, it's overwhelmingly white and English-speaking, much different from what it was like in the nineteenth century when it was a babble of native peoples, multilingual migrants, and immigrants.

Beyond Eureka is the People's Republic of Arcata, a college town and bastion of progressive environmentalism. On Saturdays in the summer, you'll usually find me at the farmers' market in the plaza, watching the hula-hoopers, jugglers, and tie-dyed hopheads swaying trance-like to Grateful Dead wannabes. A few miles north of Arcata is Trinidad, once a center of the Yurok universe, then in the mid-nineteenth century an entry point for Gold Rush speculators, later a twentieth century whaling and fishing port. Now it's mostly a stop for tourists heading north or for the few folks who can afford to look for a second or retirement home in this pricey setting.

Further north in a sparsely populated section of Humboldt County, hugging the coast, is Big Lagoon. It's the kind of place that National Geographic had in mind when it identified this area as among the top ten "unspoiled" tourist destinations in the world. I used to think that here, enveloped in rusticity, I'm somehow making an anti-commercial statement by following in the footsteps of eco-tourists who, according to a Sacramento museum, "discovered California's natural beauty in the late 1800s and early 1900s. The sparkling lakes, Alpine peaks, rapid rivers, rugged canyons, exotic animals, Native American cultures, and sandy beaches entranced them."

But look carefully and the landscape reveals that mainstream economics has had a great deal to do with the development of places like Big Lagoon. Prior to becoming generically stuck somewhere between the "exotic animals" and "sandy beaches," the Yurok lived for at least forty generations in several choice spots along the Pacific, from the Klamath River down to Humboldt Bay. For most of its social history, the area was not a refuge from the world, but where the action was. Long before Big Lagoon became a cultivated wilderness, it was home and a workplace to thousands of people.

Yurok settlements may have been sedentary and settled "since time immemorial," but this doesn't mean that they lived in a closed or static world. Prosperous towns, like the one at Big Lagoon, were a hubbub of exchange: the Yurok traveled far and wide in the northwest region, trading redwood, elk horns, and sea food for dentalia shells, obsidian, and woodpecker feathers.

In the late eighteenth century, many decades before the Gold Rush, northern California was already incorporated into regional and global economies. When

Spanish adventurers stopped at Trinidad on Trinity Sunday in 1775 in search of supplies and a northern port, they stayed nineteen days. They planted a cross as a "sign of possession" on the Indian settlement of Tsurai's highest hill and prematurely claimed "all these lands, seas, and its landmarks" in the name of Charles III and their Catholic god.

By the early nineteenth century, the Pacific was the site of multinational hunting expeditions for lucrative pelts to be sold on the China market. In June 1806, the coastal Yurok were trading otters for iron tools and other implements with the crew of a ship captained by a Bostonian, financed by Russians, and manned by indentured Kodiak and Aleut natives from Alaska. This joint venture was set up to exchange otter skins in Canton for teas, silks, spices, and nankeens. Captain Winship didn't stay long in Trinidad. He thought it "most prudent to withdraw and retreat to the ship as the natives were collecting from every quarter."

But venture capitalists returned less than half a century later and stayed this time, displacing longtime native settlements in the rush for gold. To the descendants of the inhabitants of the region, that cataclysmic moment of turmoil and warfare is sometimes referred to as "the time when the stars fell." To scholars, what happened in Northern California was emblematic, in the words of historian Tom Bender, of "the greatest human demographic disaster in the historical record."

In 1850, prospectors loaded up on provisions in Trinidad and headed up to Big Lagoon because it offered a choice of ancient trails to mining sites north or inland. One explorer witnessed his traveling companions engage in the "cowardly and wanton murder of poor naked savages" in Big Lagoon. A few weeks later, a vigilante force burned the main Yurok village and took prisoners back to Trinidad where they were executed by a firing squad. "I was associated with men who thought nothing of murder," lamented Thomas Gihon. "My heart was heavy. I had never seen such an affair before, and it made me sick at heart."

Most of the good pioneers who, unlike Gihon, dismissed the humanity of the Yurok as they stomped through the land, benefited little from their own racism. The narratives of travelers are filled with complaints and disappointments: about being price-gouged for necessities, getting sick from the rigors of "very hard traveling" along the coast and mercury poisoning at the mines, and being swindled by "speculators and charlatans" promoting the lure of "tinsel gold." The majority of adventurers who expected to get rich, noted an astute observer in the 1850s, "returned impoverished and harvested only regrets and bitterness from their most brilliant hopes."

Moreover, the Yurok did not go quietly into the past. There was resistance and survival as well as atrocities and victimization. The "Indians of the Lagoon," noted a letter in a local newspaper in 1855, "are well concealed in the redwoods and are not easily reached, if they can be reached at all." Those that survived hired themselves out as beasts of burden or went to work in canneries and the nascent lumber industry; many women lived with miners and settlers, some out of necessity or coercion, some voluntarily. The Yurok also figured out how to market themselves—first selling their specialized knowledge of the terrain to Argonauts seeking the fastest trails, where to cross rivers, and how to avoid predatory bears. Later, around the turn of the century, some sold stories and recollections to anthropologists, artifacts to collectors, and images to photographers eager to feed a nationwide nostalgia for a "vanishing race."

By the early 1860s, the Yurok of Big Lagoon and other coastal settlements were defeated by superior technology, relentless numbers, and infectious diseases. Some historians now call this encounter in northern California "genocide," but all agree with the anthropologist Alfred Kroeber that "the white man came and irreparably tore the fabric of native life to pieces." Statewide, the American Indian population was reduced by about ninety percent within a hundred years; the Yurok population declined from an estimated 2,500 in 1770 to 700 in 1910. When Kroeber visited Big Lagoon in the early 1900s, he found "all the Indians gone except one family." O-pyúweg had been "ploughed over."

Meanwhile, by the 1850s newcomers established ranches and farms in the region, some living with native women. In the late 1870s, the Big Lagoon Mining Company tried to extract gold from the sand, but quickly failed. So did other entrepreneurs who tried their luck at opening a hotel, starting a commercial nursery, and building a model town.

In the early 1920s, the small farmers and ranchers who owned land at Big Lagoon sold off their interests to corporate timber companies that occupied the area for many years to come. By the mid-1940s, the Hammond Lumber Company had set up a company village near Big Lagoon, equipped with prefabricated "bachelor cabins" and a mess hall that could serve 120 men at one sitting. The camp, noted a local newspaper, was "as modern as tomorrow."

A few years later, the nearby forest of old-growth redwoods—once so central to the Yurok economy—had been clear-cut. Not long afterwards, with the profitable extraction of trees in the area now exhausted, the lumber company sold off its Big Lagoon properties to the county and to the newly incorporated "cabin colony" known as Big Lagoon Park Company. A decade later, one of its cabins became my second home.

The pristine qualities of Big Lagoon that attracted me in the 1970s were first promoted in the 1890s when "rusticating" became popular in Humboldt. By the turn of the century, the duck-hunting season brought a thousand sportsmen to the lagoon. California's state government first got involved in marking historical sites and marketing tourist attractions in the 1920s. In southern California, a therapeutic climate, revitalized missions, and luxury hotels attracted wealthy visitors. Up north, the "redwood highway" was promoted to travelers who appreciated the rugged outdoors and wanted to witness "true living fossils."

Newton Drury, the first executive director of the Save-the-Redwoods-League (and later head of the National Park Service), played a key role in preserving what was left of old-growth redwoods as tourist attractions. When he was put in charge of the state's historical marker program in 1931, he worked closely with automobile associations and local chambers of commerce to make sure that the only places designated as historic sites, including redwood groves, would be accessible from the road.

The automobile helped to put Big Lagoon on the map. In 1929—the year that motorboat races on the lagoon attracted some three thousand spectators—the county leased land from the Little River Redwood Company to create a public park, including the construction of vacation cabins. Aside from a brief period during World War II when the area was used for military target practice, tourism and recreation gradually prevailed.

As a consequence of state-sponsored tourism, by the 1920s Big Lagoon was popular with day-trippers and campers, sportsmen, and pothunters looking for Indian "relics." Archaeologists and their surrogates also set up operations at Big Lagoon and other Yurok sites, digging up human remains and artifacts from graves for transportation to UC Berkeley in the name of science and "salvage anthropology." Then, and for the next fifty years until the creation of the militant Northwest Indian Cemetery Protection Association (NICPA), nobody paid any attention to Yurok protests. "We're not property, and neither are our ancestors," a NICPA leader told Time magazine in 1981.

In less than a hundred years, Big Lagoon's economy went from hunting and gathering to subsistence farming, to corporate capitalism, and public recreation—an accelerated version of what took centuries to develop in other parts of the world. By the time that I started visiting the area in the mid-1970s, Big Lagoon's Native American, agricultural, and commercial histories were erased. It had become the kind of bucolic retreat that folks like me were seeking as a respite from the metropolis.

But it is difficult to purge the landscape of its ghosts. The past never rests in peace; it is always in motion, subject to revision and reinterpretation. Recently, the Coalition to Protect Yurok Cultural Legacies at O-pyúweg, a successor to NICPA, was formed to repair the damage done by looting, vandalism, erosion, and amnesia. As a historian working with the Coalition, it is tempting to replace the ersatz story of Big Lagoon as an eternal recreational wilderness with one true history, or to fine-tune a synthesis out of competing narratives. But the real challenge is to remember how the tectonic layers of Big Lagoon's messy, troubling, panoramic past – formed by the present absences of natives and settlers, homesteaders and lumber barons, victims and survivors, visitors and residents, buried and excavated—continue to send shudders through the here and now.

Mark Arax

TULARE LAKE

I didn't know Tulare Lake still existed, at least not as an actual body of water. It showed up empty on my map of California, not a drop of blue anywhere. I knew a bit about its past, that it had been the biggest basin of freshwater west of the Mississippi, that it had been home to four distinct tribes of Yokut Indians, that Chinese fishermen in the late 1800s worked its water for Tulare Lake terrapin that made the finest turtle soup in the fancy restaurants of San Francisco. At its best, a century and more ago, the lake had measured 700 square miles, the most dominant feature on the California map. If you know something about the state's interior, you understand how remarkable it was to travel from Bakersfield to the San Francisco Bay on boat, hopping rivers and lakes. This was possible as late as the 1930s, before the dams stopped cold all the Sierra rivers, before the farmers dried up Tulare Lake and carved out the richest cotton patch in the world.

And so it came as some surprise that in the spring of 1998, after a heavy winter gave way to a super snowmelt, that I got a call from a friend telling me that "Tulare Lake has come back to life."

A few days later, I hopped into my car and drove for miles and miles across a flat expanse of Kings County, past vineyards and almond orchards, past dairies and alfalfa fields, until the road suddenly quit at the base of a huge earthen wall. It was a dike not unlike the dikes of Holland. The air filled with the faint smell and sound of ocean. Climbing atop the muddy embankment, gaping at the lake's big belly, I felt lost for a moment, dizzy with vertigo. Was this the heart of California cotton country or the New Jersey shore? The wind whipped whitecaps past telephone poles that displayed the high-water stains of past revivals. The lake was brown in parts and pure blue in others, and the speed with which nature had found its old self was a wonder to behold. The sun glinted off flocks of mud hens, pintail and mallard ducks, giant blue and white herons and pelicans scooping up catfish.

The lake, maybe one-twentieth of its original size, had flooded a stretch of the San Joaquin Valley that now belonged to J.G. Boswell, the biggest farmer in America and the last of California's great land barons. He, and his uncle before him, had drained an inland sea and made the rivers run backward to build their cotton empire. Chased out of their native Georgia by the boll weevil, the Boswells and other Southern growers had brought the plantation to a corner of the West in the 1920s. It was a story of astonishing vision and will and the flouting of nature, not to mention a parade of hubris.

Dams and dikes not only thwarted the four rivers that fed into the basin. The rivers themselves were no longer rivers but rather precise bands of irrigation water. Along their straitjacketed banks, the cotton giants had planted massive pumps to make sure that no water flowed where they didn't want it to flow. Even so, once every decade, and sometimes more often, a lavish snowmelt would shoot down the mountain and onto the plain, pushing past even the contrivances of Boswell. Near his hometown of Corcoran, a remnant of the old Yokut lake, a sea of ten million geese, would come back to life.

That summer, as the lake dried up once again, I heard about the old Yokut curse that went something like this: *You surely drained our lake dry, but its mists will still rise up from the tule reeds and haunt you forever.* That mist, the valley's tule fog, was our curse from late November through late January, each winter causing untold accidents on the road.

Like the lake, the Yokut were gone. I found them only in books. I learned they had built tule rafts buoyant enough to carry an entire family for days at a time on the lake and haul hundreds of pounds of rainbow trout, perch, catfish, pike and salmon—caught with bare hands or speared through a hole in the bottom of the craft. The oyster-shaped sea was so shallow, two or three feet deep in many parts and never more than forty feet at its deepest, that a fierce northwest wind would whistle through the reeds and blow the waters another mile or two across the savanna. From the shore, the women would wade in, feeling with their toes as they scoured the lake bottom for clams, mussels and terrapin. It took no time at all to fill the conical baskets slung across their backs.

To describe their world, the Yokut found language in the throats of swans and the hooves of antelope. The billy owl gave out a tiny squeak when it bobbed its head, and the human imitation of this sound, peek-ook, became the word for billy owl. The word for ducks was the gabbling noise they made while feeding, wats-wats. Tulare lake was the Pah-ah-see, the pulse of its ebb and flow. It took something different, though, to capture the sound of the blue sky as it turned dark and deafening from the wings and cries of millions of native and migratory birds—Canadian geese, mallards, swans, pelicans, cranes, teals, and curlews. How to mimic the sudden flight of flocks so immense they extinguished the sun? One of the first white men to camp along the lake could think of only one noise, the roar of the freight train, that compared with the takeoff of the birds. But the Native had no way of drawing on the railroad for inspiration. By the time the Southern Pacific arrived in the San Joaquin Valley, the land no longer belonged to the Yokut and their language had stopped breathing new words. So their word to describe the great honking sky of geese was no sound at all, but a number. *Tow-so, tow-so.* A thousand thousands.

"Los Angeles, CA Central Library 1971"

Louise Steinman

Paradise on Hope: L.A.'s Central Library

"I have always thought that Paradise was a kind of library."
  —Jorge Luis Borges

On a November morning, a crowd soaks up the wan sun in the Maguire Gardens in front of Central Library. The lucky ones sip coffee out of paper cups, others slump in the stupor of the unslept. A black feral cat slinks out of the shrubbery to forage. At a quarter to ten, the waiting throng jockeys for position at the three entrances to the Central Library: Flower Street, 5th Street, and Hope. At 10 a.m., a library security officer unlocks the tall copper doors and swings them outwards. The crowd surges inside in a race to reach computers, magazines, warmth, chairs, public restrooms.

I've worked at Central Library for sixteen years now, yet the urgency of this morning ritual never fails to move me. After all, this is no mad rush for rock concert tickets or wide-screen TVs. These people are hurrying into a *library*. This library is many things to many people—a place where scholars do serious research, where parents read aloud to their children, where jobseekers polish resumes. In the Literacy Center, volunteers tutor adults in reading, in the Popular Library, commuters peruse audiobooks and in the public restroom near the 5th Street entrance, homeless women brush their teeth.

In the Mark Taper Auditorium, where I curate a lecture and performance series, Angelenos gather to listen to a physicist discuss black holes or a novelist extol "the human fidelity to beautiful ideas." We've presented Zen archers and hip-hop poets, a panel of bloggers and journalists helped us envision the rocky future of the *Los Angeles Times*.

The Central Library was built in 1926 during one of the city's boom cycles. It may have been a time of shoddily constructed subdivisions, but the Central library was built to last. The building was a collaboration among the architect Bertram Grosvenor Goodhue, the painter Dean Cornwell, and the German-born sculptor Lawrie Lee. Goodhue's intent was to mimic Egyptian architecture: topping the library roof is a pyramid tiled on all four sides with images of the sun. At its apex is a golden hand circumscribed by the Serpent of Knowledge and holding aloft a torch: "the light of learning." The Goddess of Civilization, flanked by two black marble sphinxes, presides over the grand staircase to the rotunda. On her crown is a tiny replica of the library. Her staff rests on the back of a tortoise. On her bronze breastplate are images of Romulus and Remus, the Egyptian pyramids, the winged bull of Babylon, the goddess Shiva, a Minoan temple, a Phoenician ship, the Cathedral of Notre Dame, a Conestoga wagon, an American bison, and the Liberty Bell. From the facades of the building, bas reliefs of great philosophers and historians— Herodotus, Virgil, Socrates, da Vinci— peer down at all who enter.

The old building was a civic treasure; but it was stuffed to the ceiling with combustible material, lacked a sprinkler system, adequate ventilation and storage space for the collection. Recommendations on fixing the outdated building were doomed with the passage of Proposition 13 in 1978. On April 29, 1986 a fire (later determined to be arson) that originated in the Rare Books Room sent smoke billowing into the afternoon sky. It took over 360 firefighters from sixty companies to subdue the stubborn blaze.

In the days and weeks that followed, many librarians joined the salvage effort, working in a foot-deep toxic stew of soot, mold, and melted debris without protective gear. Many contracted a wicked chronic bronchitis from these efforts. (The perpetrators have never been apprehended.) Nearly 400,000 books were destroyed, but the disaster did have a silver lining, mobilizing the public and civic leaders to raise funds to rebuild Central Library.

In 1993, the expanded, renovated, technologically updated building opened to great fanfare. I began working there that same year, with a mandate to create public programs. In my dreams that first year, I noted in my journal, the library often appeared as a maze "with many secret areas as yet unopened to the public."

⚮

Every Thursday morning school groups visit Central Library. I watch the second graders sitting cross-legged on the marble floor of the Rotunda under the Zodiac chandelier. Their high-pitched voices blur in the vast hall. They look upwards with wonder and curiosity at Dean Cornwell's forty-foot high California history murals that cover the vaulting walls. Cornwell, a magazine illustrator, completed them in 1932. The murals are visually delightful and—if you've read much California history—intellectually distressing. Cortez steps ashore. Muscular heathens kneel at his feet, heads bowed, offering gifts of beads and pelts. "A chubby eight year old asks, "How did he paint it?" During Cornwell's lifetime, a newspaper called the Central Library murals "the largest ever executed by one man since Michelangelo decorated the Sistine Chapel."

The docent crouches down next to the boy, who is the same hue as the kneeling Gabrielino. She points out how there are over three hundred figures, each one outlined in pale blue. "Look, those are the padres, they are holding the building plans for missions. They walked the length of California."

And I am back in my own fourth grade classroom at La Ballona Elementary in Culver City, melding flour, water, salt for my relief map of my home state. We constructed California missions out of popsicle sticks and learned that the Indians were grateful to be clothed, fed, and educated by the good padres. It wasn't until my thirties, working on a documentary film about Ishi, the last Yahi Indian in California, that I learned the uglier side of California history—the forced conversions, repression of native languages, the official state bounty on Indian scalps the plunder of resources Indians needed to survive— all painfully symbolized by those subservient figures in Cornwell's murals.

There are plenty of books on the library's shelves that tell about the rich culture of California's indigenous peoples. I wonder if those second graders will someday possess the curiosity to seek them out and read them.

꒜

The library is open to all and, as the Great Recession tightens its grip, a growing number of L.A.'s homeless seek haven there during the day. The untreated mentally ill are among the regular visitors, ranting, sitting and staring, making entrances and exits through the lobby. A few weeks ago, a man attempted suicide in the library atrium. An e-mail from the City Librarian went out to all staff: "A man jumped at 11:45 a.m." No one could agree from which floor—some said the third, some the fourth. A librarian in the Literature Department caught the motion out of the corner of his eye. Some said he took a running leap, others that he stepped over the railing without hesitation. Without a doubt, he fell onto the Atrium Lower Level

One, where the first security officer to reach him was Officer Kyles, who, I happen to know, can speak in tongues. Damage was done, blood spilled, bones askew— the man barely alive. Officer Kyles stayed by his side. "Did you pray for him?" I asked later. He nodded somberly. "He wasn't going to die on my watch." The jumper did live, surviving surgery and a tenure in the ICU at County Hospital. Officer Kyles says they're trying to find his family.

Recently, as part of our lecture series, the Surrealist poet Andrei Codrescu spoke about his Posthuman Dada Guide. During his talk, it occurred to me that our jumper may have considered himself already in the posthuman world, that he'd moved on to the phase when one can exist half human, half bird.

∽

There's a charming tiled fountain flanked by tangerine trees that I walk past every day en route to work, after climbing the stairs from Hope Street. It took years until I finally noticed the quote chiseled in the marble: "Wisdom is the ripe fruit of much reflection." The converse is now etched into my mind as well: Ignorance is the unripe fruit of much inattention.

After all, for years I exited the library onto Hope Street at the end of every work day, without realizing this was the same Hope Street inscribed on my birth certificate. It wasn't until Cornerstone Theater mounted a site-specific production of *Candide* (re-titled *Candude, the Civil Servant*) in the Central Library that I made the connection. At the climax of the play, the actors lead the audience on a journey through one of the library's underground tunnels and, at the finale, the hero Candude flung open the doors onto Hope Street. "Hope!" he cried. "Here it is."

Hope Street, where I was born, just six blocks away from Central Library. I haven't come far from my origins. Perhaps that's why the idea of Central Library as a hearth of the city resonates so deeply with me. This life-quickened repository of wisdom, an un-virtual world where we daily interact with serpents of knowledge, goddesses of civilization, scholars, bodhisattvas, poets, madmen, would-be suicides. Where every morning at 10 a.m. (while there's still the budget and the public will to keep it open), the eager crowd rushes in.

"Ignition"

James Brown

TODOS NARCOS

It used to be a diner for truckers passing through San Bernardino on Interstate 10. I stopped there once with two of my boys on our way to a wrestling tournament in Colton, a rough town where Wyatt Earp once lived, the principal survivor of the shoot-out at the O.K. Corral. This was years before California passed its no smoking laws, and I remember how it hung in the air of the diner, the smoke a dense bluish haze hovering over the heads of the mostly white men seated at the counter and booths. The food was cheap and lousy.

Now it's a Mexican restaurant, and, my friend Orlando tells me, a drop-off point for narcotics. He edits a local Spanish-language newspaper, and he takes me here partly because the food is good and authentic, and partly because he wants "to break me out of my white-boy shell." My friend went to private schools and graduated from Yale. I grew up in poverty and drug-infested neighborhoods, passing high school, lucky to make it into a state university. And the better part of my life was spent getting wasted. I've been stabbed twice, had my nose broken three times, and on separate occasions a knife to my throat and a gun to my head. I've done similar to others.

Orlando stops on our way inside.

"Check it out," he says.

We stand in the parking lot. He knows how my mind works.

"Notice anything unusual?"

It's only a restaurant parking lot, but if you think about it, if you look around, you'll understand why this location was as once as ideal for truck drivers in search of a convenient spot to pull over as it is now for dope smugglers. This isn't to say that travelers and locals don't eat here, too.

Four different entrances and exits lead to Interstate 10, and Interstate 215, which branches off toward San Diego or Barstow, isn't but a few hundred yards away. Directly behind the restaurant is a hotel where you can buy a woman's time, but mostly only during the day, as night traffic attracts "heat," and that's the last thing organized narcos want. I imagine they control this trade, too. And behind the hotel, beyond the highways, is a maze of back roads and ramshackle houses. If a deal goes bad, if something goes down with the narcos or cops and you had to run, they'd have a hard time catching you.

I smile at Orlando.

"It's perfect for pick-ups and drop-offs."

"Exactly."

I point.

"And that fence over there. I don't know what's on the other side, but you could jump it and probably keep jumping."

We go into the restaurant. It's all windows. From anywhere in it you can see outside into the parking lot. It's well kept, the tables and floors clean, and at first glance you might think this would be a nice place to bring your family. But today, at least, there are no mothers with their children, no women at all other than the young waitresses whose uniforms are tight-fitting T-shirts and mini-skirts. There are only men, and I'm stared at by a few who, I imagine, might think I'm a cop. I look the part. White. Short hair. Middle-aged and middle-class and I lift weights four times a week. Orlando stands out too in his khaki pants and button-down shirt.

Mariachis, or what my friend calls a *banda*, play to a group in a booth at the back of the restaurant. Battery powered amplifiers are attached to the belts of the musicians and their instruments are electronic. The men at the booth are a mix of ages, the young one wearing white boots and a white belt. Orlando and I have to wait between songs to talk. He's as much a reporter as an editor and both often know more than they should. It's why so many journalists are killed by narcos in Mexico. And that violence, according to my friend, is spilling over the border.

"Do you know how they work?"

"No, I was just a user."

"It comes down like this," he says. "A 'mule' drives in from Tijuana in a beat-up old Toyota with a load and parks in the lot. He leaves the keys in the car. He comes inside and orders something to eat and, by the time he's finished, the car is gone. They never meet. They don't know each other, and unless he watches him take the car, which isn't a good idea, he doesn't even know what the other guy looks like."

A pretty young waitress appears at our table.

"*Yo quisiero sopa de siete mares,*" Orlando says.

I don't know if she speaks English, but I can say *pollo burrito*, and everyone understands "Diet Coke." As she leaves I watch her walk away. She has nice legs. Orlando laughs. "I knew you'd like this place." He's gay but appreciates women.

"What'd you order?"

"It's the Mexican version of crab cioppino. It's called the Soup of the Seven Seas, and it has everything in it. Oysters. Clams. Shrimp. Mussels."

Our meals are excellent, but the mariachis play too loudly so we're forced to eat without conversation. Afterwards, back on Interstate 10, I look out over the suburbs of San Bernardino. I've lived in this county, the most populous in the nation, for more than twenty-one years. I've taught at the state university here, and many things have changed.

Where billboards once advertised in English, now just as many are in Spanish. Ralph's, a local grocery store, has become a Latino market. I see the neat rows of houses built alongside the freeway, and I know, having grown up in neighborhoods like them, that they are occupied mostly with decent hard-working people just trying to make ends meet. But I know the other side, too, the scream of the woman as her husband, binging on meth, bloodies her face with blow after blow. I've been in the room and heard the cry of a newborn while the mother, sitting on the edge of the bed, slips a needle into her arm. I've heard dozens and dozens of men in the rooms of AA and NA tell of deserting their families for a fix or a drink. Over the years, I've seen countless teenage girls, children really, selling themselves on the streets to feed their habits.

But most clearly, as we pass a vacant lot off to the side of the freeway, I remember the kid I met and befriended in rehab who never made it back from his weekend furlough. He died in one of these lots, littered with trash, his face pale blue, for the face is always pale blue because junk takes you by suffocation, and I imagine his head resting on a beat-up tire, an empty syringe with his thumb still on the plunger. My former AA sponsor died the same way, only at a dope house, a week after he got out of prison. In both cases it was heroin—called "tar," *negro*, or "black" on the streets in California. On the East Coast, you get the better China White.

I think about Wyatt Earp and the shootout at the O.K. Corral, the never-ending battle between law-and-order and the desperados, only they're narcos today, and they rob lives instead of money, destroying our children, their hopes and possibilities. My friend says that the cops are just as much to blame, and I'm sure some are on the take, that some are users themselves, but in numbers they're not even close to being the enemy.

Outside, I watch a kid walk past a beat-up Ford Escort in the parking lot. He stops. He scans the area and then goes back to the car. The windows are tinted all around, and he cups his hands to the glass on the driver's side and peers between them. He is looking, I imagine, for keys dangling from the ignition.

"Anza-Borrego Desert"

Susan Straight

I went to the desert last week, to the bottom of California, the world most Americans never see, though they eat the grapes, lemons, grapefruit, fish, and dates grown in Riverside and Imperial counties. I have been coming here all my life, camping as a child in the Anza-Borrego, visiting family, or just studying all the food that comes from this naturally barren landscape. I come to remember where this bounty is grown and touched, and always, every year, I marvel at our ability to defer the truth, which is all around me, around us. Thermal and Mecca, Indio and Ripley, Calexico and Mexicali.

We face each other here, Mexico and California, in the expanse of sand and cactus and mountain that immigrants cross to enter the richest nation on earth.

According to the U.S. Border Patrol, more than five hundred immigrants have died in the San Diego and El Centro regions since October 1997. They perished of dehydration or they froze; they drowned or died in vehicle accidents. Operation Gatekeeper, begun in 1996 to seal off the border at Tijuana/San Ysidro, forced migrants toward this region, the desert.

This year alone, 376 migrants were rescued in those two sectors, most by Border Patrol agents, some by Americans and Mexican-Americans searching for lost souls on their own. Those rescued will be sent back across the border, of course. But they'll attempt to cross again. In fall, the heat still reaching over one hundred degrees, they will head here to harvest lemons, grapefruit and dates that ripen now.

The migrants might find the water tanks some Americans have placed in strategic locations to save them. Or they might find the tanks empty, since some Americans recently vandalized them, in southern California's desert counties, in anger at immigrants.

Through the canyons and arroyos of remote mountains, or in the vast expanse of land around the Salton Sea, they are led by "coyotes," the men they've paid up to $2,000 to guide them. But, often, coyotes abandon their charges, who wander the hot sand, shelter under mesquite trees and drink their own urine in desperation. Last year, fourteen people died that way in Arizona, and early this summer, seven more died southwest of Tucson. Some don't perish of thirst—they drown in the All-American Canal that I drove along, a wide blue-gray rush in cement banks on which it is impossible to gain a handhold. The canal brings water to the crops the immigrants are trying to reach, to pick, to load onto pallets and into trucks, then to unload at warehouses, or maybe to cook in restaurants.

I drove south toward Indio, the same route I follow every year, leaving Riverside behind and entering the desert. I always linger in the date groves of Indio and Thermal, then the vineyards of Mecca, skirting the Salton Sea, heading all the way to Ripley, a tiny farming town where my foster sister and brother's family lived when I was a child. I end in Calexico, the last place in California.

In the desert, almost every face on the highway was brown: vanloads of pickers, truckers moving tomatoes and grapes and citrus, and men driving old, dusty American cars. The date palm groves outside Indio were serene as cathedrals, the dangling golden fruit protected by paper bags attached by men in cherry-pickers. Then the grapevines near Mecca, where the harvest was on, hundreds of bandanaed faces and baseball caps moving up and down the rows. Down by Niland, tilapia grew in ponds tended by workers feeding the fish and cleaning the water.

I passed the brackish expanse of the Salton Sea, where my husband's relatives used to fish for corvina. His people, refugees themselves from the economic deprivation of Mississippi, settled in Calexico in 1950 because that's where their car broke down, as family legend goes. They laughed at the primary crop here back then: cotton. Some of their descendants became the first black Border Patrol agents.

In Ripley, where irrigated fields quilt the desert landscape, I drove slowly through dusty streets, past house trailers, thinking of my foster siblings' family who'd lived here in the 1960s. They were immigrants from Arkansas who'd crossed the state borders because they were hungry.

I stared out at the shimmering sand and ghostly smoke trees near the border. Before 1996, hundreds of people scaled fences and walls nightly in Tijuana and San Ysidro, all around San Diego and in other cities along the border. Now, hundreds move through the mirages hovering above the asphalt and creosote.

Along the canal, I thought, Water is inexorable, and will find another way.

Americans don't see the migrants. I have heard people react to the news of migrant deaths, or numbers of migrant crossings, or reports of Mexicans returning home to vote, by saying, "Where do these people hide? I never see them." I've heard people say, "They just come here to get on welfare, 'cause you never see them all working. They might stand on the corner selling oranges, or those overpriced flowers, but I don't see them actually working."

They haven't seen the hills outside Riverside where my mother will move into a new development. My children pointed out that Mexican men were pouring the concrete, nailing the drywall, and crawling on the roofs to lay tile.

My children always notice Mexican immigrants, possibly because my girls have brown skin and long black hair. They are often mistaken for Mexican children, admired in Spanish spoken to them by female hotel workers when we stay overnight, smiled at tenderly by restaurant workers when we are standing in a parking lot where cooks and bus people are taking a break.

I can speak Spanish, not well but politely, and they tell me they are from Zacatecas and Michoacan and Nayarit. They tell me about their own kids, or where they live now. We talk about the weather. Then they go back inside.

At restaurant chains, where the waitresses are generally American women, my children have noticed that the cooks are generally Mexican men. My girls have commented on this in Santa Barbara and Los Angeles, in New York City, in Flagstaff, and in Riverside. They are curious from overheard conversations about migrants and welfare, unkind things they've heard American parents say in school parking lots about Spanish-speaking kids.

I followed the All-American Canal back north toward Mecca then, in the early evening. People were preparing to sleep in cars, in truck beds, in motels where they crowd ten to a single room, or just on a blanket under a tree in a vacant lot. I saw men firing up tiny grills, opening beers, in a circle around dinner like the cowboys of the old movies. Except their horses were old Impalas and Broncos, and they were in the desert, in vacant lots outside Mecca.

I wondered when the men got paid. My brother, who lived in an orange grove at the edge of the city, told me he'd witnessed Mexican crews finish picking oranges or grapefruit, while the foreman called immigration on the last day. My brother watched, gathering his own grapefruit, while the men scattered through his trees or were picked up by light green INS vehicles. This way, no money for work accomplished had traded hands.

At the edge of Indio, I stopped to eat at a fast-food place where everyone behind the counter spoke Spanish, as did everyone ordering. I ate my French fries and thought about who had touched them, when they were potatoes in the dirt, when they were being sliced and frozen, when they were unpacked and fried just now.

I watched two brown-skinned kids eating hamburgers, and recalled someone from L.A. had recently told me all the nannies she knew were Salvadoran. The woman had laughed and said, "All the blond kids are speaking Spanish and eating pupusas."

It was late, and still hot in the desert, and I had to go home. I headed north again, passing the darkened date groves, the palm fronds like feather dusters against the purple sky. Two of my daughters attend an elementary school that is half bilingual. Some of the kids have been in the U.S. for years, and some kids just arrived last week.

My youngest reports that her friend Juan has to go back to Mexico for two weeks to see his grandmother, who is very ill. "She might die," my daughter says solemnly. The border seems a porous place to my children, and they wonder how people can die in the sand trying to get to the street near their grandfather's house. That's where day-laborers have gathered for years, before dawn, dozens of men glancing toward our car, checking our faces to see if we want them. They wait anxiously for contractors and landscapers and homeowners who will hire for the day.

At one vineyard, headlights were aimed toward the grapes, so people could keep picking in the cool of night. My radio was tuned to Radio Tricolor, which plays its call numbers and a signature tune proclaiming "*Mexicanisima.*" I heard songs about *mojados* who died, who lived, who sent money home but were forgotten by their wives, or who forgot their wives. Songs about migrants from Zacatecas and Sinaloa, about *la migra* and love. Bad love, good love, and lots of songs about loving a *ranchito* in Mexico, about missing home. Between the songs were commercials for Sears. "*Es su tienda.*" It's your store.

The vineyard receded in the rearview mirror, the silvery headlights pooling much brighter than the distant moon.

"Headstone for Woman"

Jenny Factor

A CEMETERY OF STONES AND STORIES:
HOME OF PEACE MEMORIAL PARK, FOUNDED 1855

Los Angeles' first Jewish cemetery, Home of Peace Memorial Park, is, at best, a misnomer. This thirty-five-acre lot rests in the tangle of two busy streets; a flat, sun-blasted rectangle dense with stones.

Here tourists come to find Fanny Brice;[1] the original Three Stooges; Russian-born slapstick producer Louis Burton; actress and singer Thelma Bernstein, who was mother to Albert Brooks; Jewish Vegas mobster David Berman; and journalist Boake Carter, a conservative commentator made famous during the Lindbergh kidnapping. Carter coined the phrase "Johnny Q. Public," and noted, quoting Aeschylus, that "the first casualty of war is truth.'"

The cemetery's first inhabitants—in 1855 in Chavez Ravine—were not permitted to rest peacefully for long. Instead, they were disinterred by members of the Hebrew Benevolent Society, a few at a time, between 1902 and 1910, and moved twenty miles east to the less in-demand, more cost-efficient corner of East Los Angeles off Whittier Boulevard.

Now, unsentimental ranks of dead stretch as far and deep as the eye can see, lined up head to head, and two-deep. The efficiencies of "making do" and the combining of different Jewish traditions of burial make an eclectic atmosphere at Home of Peace. In the cavernous Chapel of Memory,[2] the burial walls stack up nine feet high, musty and dim-lit, with names that sound of Country Club and Old Hollywood, of a life in medicine, and long middle-age afternoons spent sitting in front of a sewing machine.

---

1   originally at Home of Peace; now relocated

2   Mausoleum Chapel, dedicated in 1934 (site plaque)

Hattie Rice and Mollie Packer. Fishel and Fradel Finger. Victor L. Rosen, Max B. Aftergood, and William Trunk. Julian Bomash, who was a mason. Michael Lévy, Native of France. The Yorkshires. The Mendelsohns. Names like Polis. Renick. Vengarick. Krug. Pollack. Safir. The Armijos. The Benardos. Names of Old England and Sephardic Spain. The Anglicized Germans. The Job-Named. The Name-Changed.

Ruben Marshak, MD. A gentle soul, kindness was his way. He served as doctors do. We miss his love, we miss him too.

Fabric flowers, faded and knuckle-bent, fill out the wall-vases.

The Hebrew Benevolent Society, a social fraternity, founded in 1854 and later joined by its Ladies' Auxiliary,[3] had an eye toward Jewish culture and good works. The families and other dreamers who followed Los Angeles' eight original Jews[4] sent money to Chicago fire victims, hosted High Holiday services, helped the victims of smallpox, and knit and collected their way through the nineteenth century's dramas. And they founded a cemetery so that a Jewish murder victim (and several infant victims of smallpox) would not have to receive a secular burial.

When Harris Caspar, a storekeeper serving mining camps on the Kern River was gunned down "because he refused to sell . . . a pair of pants on credit," members of the Hebrew Benevolent Society had his remains transferred to Los Angeles for Jewish burial. Although the Benevolent Society had possession of the land near Chavez Ravine since 1854, this first burial necessitated a monetary exchange with the city— probably following the covenant by which the Biblical Abraham purchased a burial plot for Sarah. In any event, the land was re-purchased from the city for the purpose of this burial in April 1855, mere days before Easter, for the reasonable sum of $1.

Now the transferred pillars that marked family plots, little four-foot rococo columns and posts, slump drunkenly on the uneven ground.

Here are a few of their messages:

From a marble pillar in three fonts and a clear hand,

IN MEMORY OF
FLORA

3　The Ladies' Auxiliary was founded in 1870
4　Federal Census of 1850

Wife of
Moritz Laventhal
Native of W. Prussia
Died
Sept. 21, 1889
Aged 36 Years
LAVENTHAL

or from a sandstone-colored pillar, slouching west,

Erected in memory
of
ROSALIE DAVIS
who departed this life
Sept. 24, 1881
Aged 57 years
May her soul rest in peace

****

None knew her but to love her
None named her but to praise

and this gentleman, and others,

FATHER
SIEGMUND BACH
1880-1904

and a nearby gray stone too old to read, marked simply,

MOTHER

At the base of many of the stones, we find the Hebrew letters for a phrase which translates "May his or her Memory be for a Blessing." How saturated with meaning a life must have been for a mere name to serve as a blessing forever after.

The Home of Peace is not my favorite California Jewish cemetery. That honor would go to Hillside—a few blocks from where I work—where the stones are laid out around a series of grassy knolls. Folks are trimming the bushes or clipping flowers every hour of open business at Hillside.

Home of Peace, by contrast, is flat and plain—and so filled today with yesterday's dead that it's virtually abandoned by modern mourners. On a Monday, the grounds-folk are few. One can wander alone, accompanied only by the noise of brakes and a hum from the LAX flight path overhead:

Joseph Schwab
Beloved Husband and Father

Bessie Schwab
Charity was in her soul

Beloved Sister, Daughter, and Niece
Mildred Goldstein
Gone but not forgotten

Each of these three with a plate shaped like an open book.

Jewish cemeteries are known as *Beit Olamin*—homes (*beit*) of eternity. Rules for burial are few:

1. No cremation. The remains must be returned to dust whole.
2. No "graven images" (meaning no icons, no photos, no representation of anything human or divine on the stones).
3. The holy burial of suicides and people with tattoos is discouraged—but is not, at least in practice, entirely eschewed.

And in any event, these rules don't hold at Home of Peace. Ashes *do* rest in little glass cases in the mausoleum. And an entire corner of the cemetery seems to sprout up with the faces of those lost.

Corridor of Peace, Corridor of Harmony, Corridor of Eternal Life

In one section of Home of Peace, off to the side by the Eastern Avenue gate, grand red and black marbles, flecked with mica, mark the remains of contemporary Jewish *Subbotniki*, Russian and Polish émigrés who have no scruples about chiseling out the likeness of their loved ones. Photo-like and candle-lit, the faces of several children, an uncle, a beloved grandfather materialize out of rock.

One of my favorite graven-image workarounds greets visitors near the parking area.

Director and writer Mark Sandrich is buried beneath a long modern red rectangular stone, distinctively signed with his name *in his own unique hand*. His years, in block print: 1900-1945.

More recently, Frieda Sandrich, 1899-2003 has joined him. Her smaller gray stone to the side of his reads: "She knew how to make everyone feel special."

Death in Judaism is meant to provide a shift in focus, a translation from the uniqueness of the individual to the enduring language of God. One of the most ancient Jewish prayers of memory, the Mourner's Kaddish, never mentions the death of a loved one. The funeral service is prescribed and heavily ritualized—garments are torn, traditional prayers are chanted. The populousness of death at Home of Peace is as Jewish as it gets—but the stones are distinctive, quirky.

Quirky? Well, of course. Old Hollywood made its own home at the Home of Peace.

Mini-mausoleums sit facing one another on the central concrete circle—Roman and inviting as a Disneyland. Around these mausoleum markers at the sunken uneven core, in a muddy patchwork of ill-cut grass, the oldest bones and the twentieth century movie moguls are interred side by side.

And there's I.W. Hellman, who, with his uncle I.M. Hellman and cousins, extended a general mercantile business to miners, offering to buy and keep track of their gold. Farmers and Merchants' Bank prevented the over-inflation of real estate in the 1860s and 1870s, helping Los Angeles endure the national economic slumps of the late nineteenth century.

There are also the industry stalwarts—Louis B. Mayer and his brothers, Harry and Jack Warner, and both Carl Laemmles—men who made an industry, whose quirks and squabbles were famous.[5]

So, in the end, Home of Peace can't be walked or felt. It must be read.

---

5   see Gabler, Neal, *An Empire of their Own: How the Jews Invented Hollywood*, Crown Publishers, New York, 1988.

For a people of the Book, these stones are books. Stories of relationship, of passage, of fitting in, and of passing-over.

And, as in a book, my favorite of these is a love story. Halfway between the main drive and the cemetery's center, two statuary armchairs face one another in front of a tombstone fireplace. The stone chairs, marked Ethel and William, are sized right for two squirrels. The bricks of the fireplace tell a story. A brick marked 1875 describes the courtship of "two happy hearts." A brick, higher up, marked 1900 recalls "children and budding blossoms/strengthen this fireside." By 1925, life has mellowed for Ethel and William Rubin. First William dies. Ethel follows. At the very top of this stone, two birds serve as a kind of crown. The verses continue:

> Two dove-like souls united
> Under God's sheltering wings
> Empty forever stand their chairs

As remarkable as is the history of Jews in Los Angeles—from pioneer, to moneylender, to movie mogul and star—the real story here is the quiet epic of these families. Jewish families who came to Los Angeles to make themselves matter. Families whose names can still be found on marquees, on synagogue walls, in the bulletins of medical and legal journals, at the Inn of the Court, or halls of power.

And here they rest, in a place not lovely but ordinary, on stones that take patience. To find. To read. Even to believe. Translated into eternity. Standing—no longer for themselves. But for us.

May their memories be for a blessing.

REFERENCES:

Stern, Norton B. (ed.), *The Jews of Los Angeles, Urban Pioneers*, Southern California Jewish Historical Society, 1981.

Vorspan, Max and Lloyd P. Gartner, *History of the Jews of Los Angeles*, The Huntington Library Press,1970.

"Chinese Railroad Workers Near Lang"

David Kipen

LANG STATION:
WHERE LOS ANGELES AND SAN FRANCISCO
MET EACH OTHER HALFWAY

"[Oedipa] walked down a stretch of railroad track next to the highway . . . She stopped a minute between the steel rails, raising her head as if to sniff the air. Becoming conscious of the hard, strung presence she stood on—knowing as if maps had been flashed for her on the sky how these tracks ran on into others, others, knowing they laced, deepened, authenticated the great night around her. . . ."
—Thomas Pynchon, *The Crying of Lot 49*

Next to a gully, midway between Canyon Country and Agua Dulce, bordered by the 14 Freeway far off on one side and a railbed close on the other, stands a plaque. You have to look up at it, since the rutted dirt road you're parked on is several feet lower than it once was. Probably nobody except hardcore railheads and extreme California history buffs like me has ever gone looking for it. Surely only Southern Pacific linemen, teenage penny-squashers and the odd coyote have ever stumbled across it by accident. But on Tuesday, September 5, 1876, fully five thousand mostly Chinese Californians—more than today could comfortably fit in Pershing and Union Squares combined—converged here at a then-bustling stage stop, name of Lang Station.

Last year in Ohio, I met an enviable man who's won awards for writing historical signage; the Lang Station plaque is not one to start his competitive spirit racing. In prose too democratic to observe petty distinctions between fragments and actual sentences, it reads:

Lang Southern Pacific Station
On September 5, 1876, Charles Crocker, President of the Southern Pacific Railroad, drove a gold spike to complete his company's San Joaquin Valley

line. First rail connection of Los Angeles with San Francisco and transcontinental lines.

Registered Historical Landmark No. 590

Plaque placed by California Park Commission in cooperation with Historical Society of Southern California. . . .

Let Utah keep its Promontory Point, where, seven years earlier, the Union and Central Pacifics cinched their steely knot with a shaft of gold. Just please save me that spike from Lang Station—where, for a few hours in 1876, Northern and Southern California put aside their beloved internecine bickering and completed a circuit connecting the City of St. Francis with the City of Angels.

Why did the two segments of the trans-California railroad join up so far from San Francisco, and not nearer its midpoint? Mostly for the same reason the two ends of the Transcontinental Railway met in Utah, and not in the Middle West: Progress steams faster with the breeze of civilization at its back. Also, as John Muir could have told the rail barons: California mountains take some getting over. Southern California has two ranges worth, the Tehachapis and the San Gabriels. Each runs rudely west-east, perpendicular to the Southern Pacific's ravenous vector.

The SP, remember, grew out of the Union Pacific, brainchild of four men: not just Crocker but ex-Governor Leland Stanford (also present at Lang Station that day in 1876), Mark Hopkins (absent, already suffering the health problems that would kill him inside two years), and Collis P. Huntington, already spending more time in the East lobbying and fleecing Congress than in the West cutting ribbons. Huntington's empire stretched from coast to coast by then, even into the hollers of West Virginia, where, not long before, the notorious track-per-day quotas on his Chesapeake & Ohio had likely killed the model for steel-drivin' John Henry.

One way and another, transportation flowed rumbling through the blood of all the Big Four. They were New Yorkers, their parents drawn there by the Erie Canal's mercantile promise: Crocker born in Troy, Stanford from nearby Watervliet, Hopkins not far away in Henderson, and Huntington, born in Connecticut but tasting his first success as an Oneonta dry-goods man. Come 1849, they smelt the gold a generation before they saw the spike.

If you can believe the Los Angeles Star's correspondent, Col. Crocker kept it short that day in 1876: "'Gentlemen of Los Angeles and San Francisco, it has been deemed best on this occasion that the last spike to be driven should be of gold, that most precious of metals, as indicative of the great wealth which will flow into the coffers of San Francisco and Los Angeles when this connection is made, and is no mean token of the importance of this grand artery of commerce which we are about to unite with this last spike. This wedding of Los Angeles with San Francisco is not a ceremony consecrated by the hands of wedlock, but by the bands of steel. The speaker hopes to live to see the time when these beautiful valleys through which we passed today will be filled with a happy and prosperous people, enjoying every facility for comfort, happiness and education. Gentlemen, I am no public speaker, but I can drive a spike!"

Drive it he did, though not too deep for hasty retrieval. Today that spike reposes in the vaults of the California Historical Society in San Francisco. It weighs nine and a quarter ounces, is five and seven-sixteenths inches long, bears this engraving along its four sides: "Last Spike . . . Connecting Los Angeles . . . And San Francisco . . . By Rail."

Within our lifetimes, lobbied and counter-lobbied by Huntington's inheritors down to this very route, a high-speed locomotive is coming over these tracks that may get you from Downtown Los Angeles to San Francisco faster than your car will get you from L.A. to Malibu at rush hour: two hours and twenty-seven minutes. Start watching *There Will Be Blood* as the train pulls out of Union Station, and you'll be off the rails before the movie is.

Even then, when skink-blue bullet trains flash by on the Sylmar-to-Palmdale run, this disused siding may not look much different from how it does now. Somewhere underfoot, shaky steps over gravel-strewn ground from the Lang Station plaque, lies the ordinary steel spike that took the gold one's place. Not many acres in California are less trod than they used to be, but this is one.

"Rock Light"

David St. John

LIGHT:
SUNRISE AND SHADOW, MAJESTY AND MENACE—HOW VERY L.A.

As a California native, I think my senses come hardwired to recognize the most subtle oscillations of California light. I know the flattened blank light of summer in the San Joaquin Valley, where I grew up. I know the rich, densely foliate light of Marin County and the hills above Santa Cruz, where I loved to spend time in my early adult years. But most of all, I react to the almost tectonic shifts of Southern California light, to the delicate rumblings of daily light, and to the delicious after-shock of that light.

In his book *David Hockney by David Hockney*, the artist talks about the struggle in painting the now-famous *Portrait of an Artist (Pool with Two Figures)*— in finding the right approach to capture the light that reflects along the surface of the pool. His description is a brilliant mini *ars poetica* of artistic process, replete with the urgency and uncertainty that come with the making of genuine art. We're all familiar with the extraordinary effects of Hockney's solution: those intersecting, remarkably delicate, witty, and snaky white lines that branch over the surface of the canvas, signifying the constantly rippling reflections of light along the water. When I first saw the painting, I felt breathless, as if those ripples implied not simply the movement of water but the movement of consciousness itself. Aha, I thought, as I looked at Hockney's painting, there's what living in California can do for you!

(Okay, a little melodramatic.)

Looking at those lines on the water assemble into a wavering white net, I understood that light is also a vehicle of memory—that it seines our past, often pulling up those dark elements (that we've previously pushed aside) into a clarifying if sometimes withering view. Light can trick us into revealing or recalling moments we've tried to forget: the way a certain angle of honeyed light cascading off a wall might call up not an ecstatic vision but instead the image of a first family death, or the split second before a lover turned and walked away, or the thick, suffocating nausea just as one's motorcycle skids to hit that honeyed wall. Memories are inscribed indelibly by the shifting details, the carved natural filigree of the light in which they first occurred.

Of course, there are many aspects to Southern California light. There is the sheer chiseling quality of the light as it reflects off the buildings in Century City. There are those exquisite panels of emerald embroidery as the sunlight filters down through the needles of the pines and firs and the loose fingers of eucalyptus in the canyons and hills surrounding the Los Angeles Basin. There is the clatter of light that ricochets along the freeways. There is the parfait of light that rises off the Pacific. There is the solitude of the light that arrives along the waves at sunset, and its somewhat ironic patience with our sentimental voyeurism; and always, the swirling of the diffuse early-morning light along the beaches and the avenues almost anywhere in the city. I can't help feeling there is a sense of permission to the light here, as the body builders, sun worshipers, beach-party devotees, and other '50s icons repeatedly told us.

In his memorable article "L.A. Glows," journalist Lawrence Weschler described the light here as both revealing and concealing. Which is to say, it's not only a light that makes visible the world around us but also a light in which objects can seem hidden, as if behind a scrim or veil. This seems to me to explain a lot about how we sometimes behave as citizens of Los Angeles. Let's face it, many of us walk around as if we were hiding in plain sight. We can sometimes feel that we are chameleons who've been granted invisibility by those white sheets of light unfolding around us, those rippling curtains of sunlight from which we believe we can emerge at any moment to take our rightful place upon some private and specially chosen stage.

The exposure we can feel in the face of such penetrating light often forces us to take up simple if sometimes elegant masks, feigning anonymity, almost like Venetians at Carnival. (As everyone learns, being who you are can be bloody awful, but not being who you are can be very sexy.) In L.A. our masks are called sunglasses, and we use them to conceal and protect more than just our eyes. Many of us—perhaps especially the actors here—lead public lives. Dark glasses help give us the illusion, however briefly, that we are or can be anonymous. We all spend so much time being somebody that once in a while we just need to be nobody. A friend's new Isaac Mizrahi sunglasses are the black, thick-rimmed, flattened-oval, near cat-eye sunglasses that one saw Brigitte Bardot and Jackie Kennedy wearing in the early '60s, usually with a scarf wrapped around their heads, when they thought they could pass unnoticed in a crowd. (We all know how well this worked from their many photos in this "disguise.") Her sunglasses are raccoon-like, bandit-like, but with the eyeholes them-selves blacked out by the impenetrable tint of the lenses. The effect is something like Park Avenue meets Zorro, but it's also completely and irrevocably L.A.

Architect Antoine Predock talks about the light of the desert as "stabbing." Near the ocean, though, he says, the light "falls and falls, and when it arrives it lands." For Predock, it's that palpable sense of passage that makes Southern California light both a physical revelation and a thing of no small miracle. That physical palpability touches us all, though at times it can also be a cruel light.

We've all learned this in recent years, but some of us have had to confront a more intimate knowledge of the sun's expense. My father lived his life out of doors, a real jock, and it is not an exaggeration to say he truly lived to play tennis. He spent as much of every day as he could—he was a teacher—on the tennis court. Summers, out of school, he played tennis twice a day. Over the course of his life he had, I would estimate, more than two hundred skin cancers removed from his body, mostly small, but some frighteningly large. In the end, of course, the melanomas caught up with him. From the time he was a young man he'd believed in the life of the body as it is lived in the open air and in the sunlight, and he came of age in a time when the perfect tan held significant meaning. Even after he knew better, it was an ideal he would never entirely discard.

Yet this love of the light has been a defining inheritance. In an early, and, for me, unusually autobiographical poem titled "Of the Remembered," a poem that ends looking ahead to my father's death, I began the first section with these lines: "I grew up in California / Where everyone stood a little closer / To the sun." It delights me to say these lines are now carved in stone in the lobby of the Junipero Serra State Office Building in downtown Los Angeles, as what poet doesn't want to be outlived by a few of his or her own words. Perhaps even more relevant, it's also comforting to know that my young daughter and grown son will be able to visit those words one day when I've finished my own brief time walking through this familiar landscape of California light; and they will know that I believed it was the most gracious and consoling and benevolent of any of our worldly lights.

"Light: Sunrise and Shadow, Majesty and Menace—How Very L.A." was first published in *Los Angeles Magazine*, © 2000, 2010 David St. John. Used by permission of the author.

Rob Roberge

Room No. 8, at the Joshua Tree Inn

I'm writing this from Twentynine Palms, California, where a few years back, my wife Gayle and I bought a cabin to get away (very away) from it all. We spend our days hiking Joshua Tree National Park, walking and driving around to and visiting the hundreds of abandoned homesteader shacks, playing guitar and singing on the porch, writing, reading and doing as much of nothing as possible. It's a great place—still something of a well-kept secret.

People come out to Joshua Tree for many reasons, but the major ones are: to go to the national park, to be in the presence of so much beauty and peace and quiet, to spot UFOs at Giant Rock, to scout the best location for their new meth lab (the city's a better bet for you Junior Achieving speed freaks out there), and to do what we do in the staggering heat of our porch: Nothing much.

And people stay at the Joshua Tree Inn, about fourteen miles west of our place, for all these reasons, plus one very specific one.

To stay in room no. 8.

Because, as many know, evidenced by the waiting list, room 8 is where, on September 19, 1973, Gram Parsons, relaxing after having finished his second solo album, the classic, although laden with too many slow-as-molasses tunes, *Grievous Angel*, died. He was an amazing singer. Listening to Gram Parsons' cracked beauty of a voice dance over a seventh chord is one of the most painfully gorgeous sounds that has ever been captured on recording equipment. There were singers with better chops, to be sure. Though, as my friend John points out, Doc Severnson had better chops than Miles Davis, who couldn't play in the upper register. Chops are never the whole story when you're talking about art.

The thing Gram Parsons had is what all great artists have—he wasn't cool or ironic. He was willing to stand metaphorically naked and stripped bare to the essential emotions. And, he could sing like no one else before or since. As someone once said, everybody switches from C to F, but nobody does it quite like Keith Richards. And nobody sounds like quite like Gram Parsons.

He died when he was twenty-six. We are past the thirtieth anniversary of his death, which means people have been missing Gram Parsons from this Earth longer than he was on it.

The circumstances surrounding his death and burial have been told and retold (most recently mistold in the so-so indie film *Grand Theft Parsons*), but I'll offer a brief summary here to those who don't know them. If you do, skip ahead.

Gram Parsons' stepfather, by most accounts an oily and brutally self-interested man, tried to rush GP's body to New Orleans for burial. There was some Louisiana loophole that would allow Bob Parsons to claim Gram as a New Orleans resident and thereby get his hands on the rather lucrative Parsons estate.

Phil Kaufman, a road manager /friend/hanger-on to Parsons and, among others, the Rolling Stones, stole the body, with help from friend Michael Martin, from LAX, where it was waiting to be shipped to Louisiana. His reasoning was simple: Parsons had told Phil Kaufman earlier that year at Clarence White's funeral, that he wanted to be cremated in his beloved Joshua Tree, where he had spent so much time.

Kaufman and Martin then, in an alcohol and drug-induced haze, drove Parsons to somewhere around his beloved Cap Rock in Joshua Tree National Park (then known as the Joshua Tree National Monument in its pre-national park days), poured gas over the coffin and lit it on fire. They high-tailed it out when Kaufman (mistakenly, it turned out) saw park rangers chasing them. The half-charred coffin was discovered the next morning by hikers (and reported as a "big burned log"), and the remains of the cremains were then shipped to New Orleans, where a dying Bob Parsons claimed and buried them.

And now, every year, people come to stay in room no. 8, where the sad and brilliant life of Gram Parsons came to such an early end. The question is, why?

There's maybe the easy reason of people being obsessed with celebrity. But that misses the boat on a couple of scores. One is that Gram Parsons wasn't that famous, or that much of a celebrity (at least not when he was alive). He was a great singer/musician, but he wasn't that popular in his lifetime. Jim Croce was scads more popular, and he died the same week as GP, and yet no one goes to whatever small airstrip it was over which Croce died. There is no pilgrimage to the flat where Jimi Hendrix died (of course, not many people die in a bed-and-breakfast, as GP did, where it's kind of convenient to pay your respects).

People are macabre, make no mistake. Henry Ford reportedly had the last breath of Thomas Edison sealed in a jar (which lead to all sorts of gruesome deathbed breath-collecting images) so there may be the ghoulish desire to capitalize in whatever personal way on someone's death. It's a tenuous analogy, the Ford/Edison thing, and the staying in room no. 8, but maybe it's a way of claiming the dead as our own when we have these personal rituals after they've left.

I'm thinking it's not for such seedy reasons that people come and stay in room no. 8 and walk around Cap Rock, where Gram Parsons' ashes are said to have been scattered. And sing sad GP songs on their porch in Twentynine Palms like Gayle and I do all the time. I'm thinking, maybe, there's a sincerity of purpose at work here.

There's an old folk tale a friend told me one time about a squirrel and a lion. The lion, after a relatively short chase, had caught the squirrel in its mouth. The squirrel said, "I know you're going to kill me, but would you let me down for just a second beforehand?" The lion did. The squirrel thrashed around in the sand, and then said, "OK." The lion asked what that was all about. The squirrel said, "I know you're going to kill me, but at least now, people will come by here and see my marks and know that I struggled."

Gram Parsons had, by most accounts, a tough life with many demons. Which doesn't make him unique. But Gram Parsons, whatever else he did or didn't do, left some of the most beautiful signs of all of our futile struggles in the sand. And maybe that seems to matter somehow, listening quietly to your own breath inside room no. 8, while the high desert winds swirl outside, much like they probably did on the night of September 19, 1973.

Lillian Vallee

River of Rebellion

We are standing in the cool shade of venerable cottonwoods and oaks in Caswell State Park. Tall nettles, golden currant and blackberry crowd the prickly understory and wild grape tendrils reach for sunlight in the dense growth of a riparian gallery forest. My companion, Tamara Glanzer, marvels at the jungle lushness in the Central Valley heat: "So much for the image of the Valley as a desert," she says.

We are here to visit the river and to find a historical marker. One hundred and eighty years ago, almost to the day, on balmy May days like the ones we are enjoying now, a Yokuts Indian named Cucunuchi (baptized as Estanislao in Mission San Jose by the president and prefect of all the missions, Padre Narciso Duran) staged a rebellion on a bank of the river that later came to bear his name: *Rio Estanislao* or the Stanislaus River.

Few of us spend any time thinking about why our county is named after an Indian leader, equal in stature and magnetism, some scholars say, to leaders such as Tecumseh or Pontiac. Estanislao had made such a powerful impression on the Mexican soldiers sent to flush him out of his forest stronghold that they began to refer to the river and the surrounding area, with some trepidation, as "the territory of Estanislao."

It is difficult to imagine the merciless speed with which history struck California Indian communities in our area. A mere two decades before the battles on the Stanislaus, Gabriel Moraga had been the first white explorer, and he renamed the river (known as the Laquisamne to the Yokuts who lived there) after Our Lady of Guadalupe. Two decades after the rebellion against the Mexican military in 1829 came the Gold Rush. The course of events is heartrending. Local journalist-historian Thorne Gray concluded the preface to his meticulous account with these words: "Future scholars and writers will finish this task. If some of them are natives, they will tell this story better than I. May we then cry together."

In Modesto we are reminded of a long struggle whenever we pass Betty Saletta's sculpture of Estanislao outside the County Courthouse. The figure's expression is grave; his hand is extended in a gesture calculated to stop, to fend off, to protest, or perhaps simply to make us consider why he has reappeared on a site devoted to matters of justice.

The Mexican army needed three forays into Estanislao's territory to dislodge insurgents. A young ensign, Mariano Vallejo, parlayed the third sortie into a career-maker in spite of having killed old women and removed children for distribution as servants and slaves. Mexican authorities in California feared that Estanislao would stage a major uprising against the entire mission system undergoing a half-hearted secularization. Estanislao would have understood that the Indians were not going to be given back the rich mission lands they had labored on and been promised. As chief producers of the hides and tallow, the currency of the day, the missions continued to support the presidios and regional governments.

Estanislao was educated by Padre Duran, about whom Captain August Duhaut-Cilly said in 1827, ". . . no soul ever held less joy than that of Fray Narciso." The date may have had something to do with it. Under pretext of a visit to his home place, the esteemed Estanislao defects and takes four hundred neophytes with him, a move deeply distressing to Duran.

Duhaut-Cilly reports that during his visit, Fray Duran predicted the end of the world, and in some ways he was right. The mission system met its end in 1831 with the ouster of Governor Manuel Victoria, "a vigorous opponent of secularization." California was in turmoil, but the native populations continued to lose ground no matter what they did: they could convert or run, intermarry or not, conform or rebel. The land grab was on and philosophy became its handmaiden.

Estanislao would have witnessed nightmarish scenes: an inhumane work regimen, severe punishments meted out for disobedience. Disease, poor nutrition, and hangings decimated his community. As an *alcalde*, an overseer and person of authority at the mission, he would have been in charge of enforcing mission rules and timetables among his people. It was not unusual for *alcaldes*, well-versed in the workings of the mission and the military, to become leaders of insurgencies when Indians rebelled or fled to the interior, to *el valle de los tulares*, the impassable tule marshes covering four million acres of the Central Valley. Valley Indians had a reputation for troublemaking and "insolence."

Estanislao's fortifications on the Stanislaus were brought down with the tool of New World conquistadors: fire. Cortez had burned the aviaries of Tenochtitlan to demoralize the Aztecs, and Vallejo set fire to the riverine jungle of the Laquisamne.

Estanislao was never captured. He returned to the mission and gained pardon from the embattled Governor Echeandia, "the first governor of California under the Mexican republican constitution," who lasted exactly four years (1825–1829). Not only were the Indians "restive" during his short tenure, so were his unpaid soldiers in Monterey. He resigned, profoundly discouraged.

Back at Caswell, we run into State Park Ranger Michael Whelan making his rounds. He informs us that the plaque we are looking for has been stolen and probably recycled for cash. He is kind enough to make us a color copy of a photo with the inscription. The heavy rock to which the plaque was bolted is still there, however; on it we leave a mugwort leaf, a bitter herb said to dispel bad spirits.

Sources: Walton Bean & James Rawls, California: An Interpretive History; August Du-haut-Cilly, A Voyage to California, the Sandwich Islands, and Around the World in the Years 1826-1829; Thorne B. Gray, Stanislaus Indian Wars; James D. Hart, A Companion to California; Stanislaus Stepping Stones, Volume 1, December 1976, Number 1; Naida West, Eye of the Bear.

Tim Z. Hernandez

Geofluvial Morphology of the San Joaquin River: A Letter to the Gardner

Dear Eliseo,

I was thinking yesterday about the question you once asked me, on how a river gets its shape. Here is what I know: It starts *somewhere*, though where exactly, no one really knows. The rain, back to rain again, down to the crown of the Sierra Nevada highlands, into snow, then at some point we get close enough to fire season and it liquefies and runs off down into the hipbone crevice of the western ridge that rolls back into the torso of the San Joaquin Valley, or *el Valle de San Joaquin*, or Valley of Saint Joachim, a brown body wrapped in a thin blue rebozo of constellations and concern. This is Yokut territory, you see, where herculean sycamores still muscle up against the flow along the banks, where salmon once danced their way from the Pacific rim up toward the redwoods. Really, who's to say anymore what is natural or what is man-made when even the stone mortar grinding holes are challenged by Jokie and Torch's aerosol brigade; graffitied slabs of sediment and boulder speckle the sacred pathways at Lost Lake Park, where the locals frequently ask, what lake?

Last week a Hmong family asked me about the ghosts of Lost Lake and I told them they're everywhere. So much has been lost here, forgotten or stripped, yet it still remains. The water is a ghost, as are the Tule Elk, and, of course, the salmon, too, gone. The family then performed a dragon ceremony before entering our canoes. Ceremony atop ceremony arrives here, and who's to say this isn't what causes the dam to flex or overflow every few years, made to wash out the encroaching invasive species? Because, on the river every day is a battle between native and non-natives True, the arundo's roots run deep, but when Tachi bluesman Lance Canales sang "Oh, San Joaquin, San Joaquin" while on the banks of the river in his hard oak voice, the people heard it like a novena, and the next morning they released water from the dam and it rose to 1,500 cfs and this changed little, but it changed, *hermano*.

146

Months later, I sat in the sand at Fort Washington Beach, off Rice Road, and had a conversation with a great blue heron. The old crone lifted her tattered gullet up toward me, then took a few steps, then a few more, and she stood there, defiant, watchful, waiting for my departure, and then I lifted a river rock and realized then what she had been wanting to tell me all along. That I could lift such a rock on the floor of a river should be answer enough. The water itself winds down from above the old mining town of Friant, beyond the fish hatchery. Used to be that same mercurial flow irrigated the whole of the Central Valley. Remember how, as children, we used to swim in the ditches in cut-off shorts, shirtless, just dove right in after a long summer day of spreading grapes with our parents, or pulling cherry tomatoes from Barnheart's farm? Now the water gets piped down to Bakersfield and Delano and the other obscure *campitos* who pray it isn't contaminated by the time it reaches their *albondiga* stew, like it did not so long ago.

The farmers, from Madera to Fresno to Orosi to Five Points, all had a good run of it in the early days. Gargantuan siphon pipes can still be found in the river's bone-yard, near the cove below Millerton's waistline; it once flowed down each narrow irrigation trench, thousands of them sprawled out over the land like Japanese Zen gardens, slaked to perfection, tilled and prayed over, and still earlier, the immense belly-scraping of cargo ships that carried the likes of Twain and his river-faring cohorts, along with drilling machines and other merciless machinations, squeezed through these valley walls by river and high flow, between what is now Valley Children's Hospital and the Eyeball Saloon, float remnants of river bank, stones and loosened driftwood, license plates and tires, a flotilla chiseling away at the lines and memories, forming corners where no such corners exist.

A river is about curvature because water moves where land is impressionable; man forces the impression, proves the point, thus all straight edges are man-made. The dam sits like a stone sky and imagines something about control and release, while the river continues its culture of flow, understanding that in the words of the great Valley poet, Juan Felipe Herrera, "no power is the power." And then, finally, last week it all came to light. While hiking a trail up at the gorge, I witnessed an unidentified snake face to face with a king snake, and the two opened their mouths and howled at one another in that silent way that snakes do, and then the king snake calmly unhinged its elastic jaw and swallowed its challenger whole, for a moment taking on this new shape, before returning to its former self. The elbertas are ripe these days, *hermano*. Find one, sit down bankside, and enjoy.

Siempre,
Tim

"Women Dancing on Rock"

Janet Fitch

DENISHAWN AND THE DAWN OF MODERN DANCE

When I was a sophomore at Fairfax High in 1971 there were two ways to get out of gym class. The first was marching band but, alas, I played no instrument. The second was a sleeper—a program of barefoot modern dance.

How many non-athletic, gym-hating freaks and hippies do you think could squeeze into the gym? Answer: at least sixty.

We gathered under the instruction of Rose Gold, a pixie-ish '50s Greenwich Village beatnik who cajoled, inspired and bullied her variously talented students through the fundamentals of the dance vocabulary. Words like "contraction" and "core work" seeped into our conversation. More important, she managed to convey the idealism of modern dance, the sheer raw joy of translating a piece of music into physical motion. For a Type-A honors student like myself, this was a gift beyond imagining—to create not from the head but from the body and the spirit.

At the time, it never occurred to me to wonder about the origin of this innovative program. It was only later, while researching a book set in Los Angeles in the early '20s, I came upon the answer: Denishawn.

The creation of Ruth St. Denis and Ted Shawn, Denishawn was both art and ethos, a phenomenon which established the pair as the mother and father of modern dance in America, with California as its natural home.

The progressive era at the dawn of the twentieth century saw people shrugging off Victorian constraints. Clothing reform for women, a fascination with the Far East and the philosophies of vedanta, anthroposophy and Christian Science were all in vogue. And Ruth St. Denis absorbed it all. A "skirt dancer" from rural New Jersey and a Belasco discovery, her particular brand of non-balletic "free dancing" reflected a desire to translate the idealism of the new era into movement and spectacle.

Like her fellow-pioneers, Americans Isadora Duncan and Loie Fuller, St. Denis took her burgeoning art to Europe's stages and salons. There, her fluid style and the high tone of her dancing took away some of the scandal from her barefoot choreographies. Unlike Isadora Duncan, who advocated a Greek simplicity, speed, and extension into space, St. Denis favored the internal, the spiritual, and the theatrical, embodied in lavishly-executed sets and costumes.

The only one of the three who returned to America, St. Denis created a new audience for dance, an audience enraptured by her mystical journeys to exotic lands. Chinese dances, undersea ballets, Egyptian tableaux and Babylonian rituals, sprang from eclectic inspirations as far-ranging as statuary, paintings, book illustrations and, even in the case of her ballet, *Egypta*, an image in a cigarette ad.

In 1911, St. Denis discovered California. Performing in San Francisco at the end of a coast-to-coast tour, she fell in love with the state, its large Asian population and its voracious appetite for mysticism and spiritual quest. Dancing throughout the state, she finally settled in Los Angeles, where she was said to be studying Japanese movement under the tutelage of a former geisha.

Three years later, Ted Shawn, a young divinity student-turned-dancer orchestrated a meeting with St. Denis. The recognition between the two idealists was instantaneous. St. Denis invited Shawn to join her dance company. By the third stop in the tour, Shawn had proposed. He was young—twenty-three to her thirty-five—handsome and iron-willed. A longtime feminist, St. Denis wavered, then assented, though she famously struck the word "obey" from the vows, and refused to wear a wedding ring. The name Denishawn was forged on that legendary tour, the serendipitous result of a publicity stunt.

The newlyweds bought a former estate overlooking Los Angeles and opened the Denishawn School, where Shawn taught ballet and ballroom dance on the outdoor stage, while St. Denis lectured on philosophy and spirituality—and conducted its famous moonlight yoga classes under the aromatic eucalyptus. Students cooled off after class in the school's swimming pool, and scandalized neighbors by chasing the St. Denis peacock onto a public road in a state of "undress."

Denishawn was more than a dance school—it was a way of life, a product of California. True to the spirit of the progressive era, it was a utopian vision of art education shared not just by Shawn and St. Denis, but by educators of the time. It proposed dance as an artistic and spiritual cure for the ills of modern, mechanized life. This philosophy became one of the basic tenets of modern dance, a California-bred linking of dance and spirit that, so many years later, the elfin Miss Gold would pass it on to my misfit, egghead self in a high school gymnasium.

In 1916, the Denishawn school included among its pupils another misfit—an "older student" from the Cumnock School of Expression in Los Angeles, the twenty-two-year-old Martha Graham. Ted Shawn recognized the fire and passion beneath her awkward shyness and recruited her for the company. The following year, St. Denis plucked the talented Doris Humphrey from the ranks of visiting teacher-students.

Another kind soon became associated with Denishawn. Studios sent their leading ladies to Denishawn to learn emotional expression through movement. Today, to watch rare film footage of Ruth St. Denis simply handling a peacock feather is to recognize the style of gesture which marked female acting of the silent era. Lillian and Dorothy Gish, Florence Vidor, and Mabel Normand were all Denishawn regulars. Louise Brooks famously became a member of the touring company, before she was kicked out for insubordination.

Soon, Denishawn outgrew its Los Angeles estate. Artistic differences between Shawn, the businessman, and St. Denis, the visionary, generally settled in Shawn's favor, and the company moved to larger quarters near Westlake Park (now McArthur Park). Meanwhile, workmen began construction on a four-hundred-seat outdoor theater in Eagle Rock. There, advanced students performed Monday Night concerts under the stars, as well as weekly children's matinees. Each step deepened Los Angeles's fascination with modern dance and the city's involvement with all things Denishawn.

With its very success, tensions grew within the partnership. The cozy domesticity of life in Eagle Rock and the mechanics of business ill-suited St. Denis, and when Shawn entered the Ambulance Corps in WWI, St. Denis toured without him, returning to the source of her own artistry—the mystic and the experimental.

When the war ended, there was a showdown between the two concerning the future of Denishawn, and Shawn opened his own studio with Martha Graham as his assistant—and St. Denis made plans for a new troupe of her own, with Doris Humphrey at its heart. She remained in L.A. while Shawn moved across the country to New York. But it soon became clear that they were more popular together, and St. Denis began touring with Shawn's company, replacing Martha Graham in many of the dances.

Today, it's difficult to imagine the scope of the Denishawn phenomenon. There were Denishawn films, a Denishawn magazine, and authorized branches of the school in a dozen American cities. Denishawn sent mail-order courses nationwide— the

Ampico piano roll company carried music for the Denishawn technique classes. For an entire generation, Denishawn was the face of highbrow dance at its most accessible.

Yet even at its apex, the end was already in sight. In the opinion of St. Denis, the New York enterprise drained income from the Los Angeles school, while Shawn wanted to focus solely upon a Denishawn community in rural New York.

In the end, it was the Great Depression which robbed Denishawn of its power to inspire. Audiences, now more cynical and sophisticated, preferred the work of such Denishawn protégés as Doris Humphrey, Charles Weidman, and Martha Graham, with their focus on the kinetic and psychological rather than the mystical. The second generation of modern dance in America was born.

St. Denis and Shawn never divorced. However, they separated in 1931 and never lived together again. Shawn formed a company of all-male dancers, and founded the monumental Jacob's Pillow dance festival, while St. Denis returned to Los Angeles and devoted herself to experiments with religious dance.

In the decades to come, Denishawn would in some way touch every great dance company in America. Merce Cunningham was a Martha Graham protégé, as was Paul Taylor, while José Limon studied with Doris Humphrey and Charles Weidman. Twyla Tharp studied with all three. Humphrey not only became the artistic director of the Limon dance company, she founded the influential dance programs at Bennington College and at Julliard, while Bob Fosse studied choreography with Weidman.

Not only did Denishawn give rise to these influential figures in American dance, it left behind the legacy of California as a dance incubator, a spiritually adventurous place where artists can invent something absolutely new. Lester Horton felt it in the '30s when he chose Los Angeles over New York, and he passed that spirit of innovation along to his protégés, dance greats Bella Lewitzsky and Alvin Ailey.

As for my magical Rose Gold, what brought her to Los Angeles to teach at Fairfax High School? Was it the lingering aroma of Denishawn incense? I think it likely. And that Fairfax High dance program—how far did its roots reach? Whichever came first, the dance program chicken or the Rose Gold egg, it was clearly the product of California's modern dance heritage and its unique Denishawn roots.

Seth Greenland

SALTON SEA

You head south from Indio on the Sonny Bono Memorial Highway. An endless freight train rumbles by, railroad cars the color of dried blood, bleaching in the winter sun. The Chocolate Mountains loom beyond the train, the confectionary name belied by their unyielding, hardscrabble planes. But on your right, bursting with vivid life, are acres and acres of lush green groves of date palms ringed by parched desert. You conjure golden camel caravans, the evanescent image of a white-robed, whirling T.E. Lawrence, his garments buoyed by the desert winds, infinity painted in sand.

A few miles past this Arabian oasis, a mirage materializes. The bluest of blue, vast and glassy, it extends toward the distant horizon. The low hills to the west are an afterthought, the eye drawn to the endless south, the vanishing point, the boundless desert landscape that is not sand and rock and scrub but shimmering water. The Salton Sea should be an illusion glimpsed through tired eyes, perceived as some kind of awesome *trompe l'oeil*, but it is as real as the mountains that cradle it, as real as the cumulonimbus clouds reflected in its cerulean depths. Saltier than the ocean, it is California's largest lake, fed by the cool waters of the Colorado River and disappearing a little each day. But there it is now, for your amazement and delectation, nature's sideshow: step right up.

You turn right on a spur off the highway and drive into the desert town of Bombay Beach, a mile square of muddy roads lined with dilapidated trailers mounted on cinderblocks. You are 228 feet below sea level. There is a rundown community center and a cracked asphalt basketball court fighting a losing battle with the tentacles of nature. The town has a moon station quality that comes with being a beach community in the middle of the Mojave. It's been said that when the Big One arrives and splits the state of California from the American mainland, Arizona will

153

be beachfront. In this future light, Bombay Beach can be seen as a post-apocalyptic harbinger of a time when the desert and the ocean blend their DNA and the strange becomes everyday. Two guys with beer guts stand next to a pickup truck in front of the general store. Beneath this anodyne surface, Bombay Beach is as incongruous as the Salton Sea itself, a two-headed chicken, bearded lady of a town.

You continue south toward Calexico. Outside of Niland, you slow down at a roadblock set up by La Migra. The expressionless officer, baking like a tortilla on the hot asphalt, nods and waves you through. At the side of the road, a teamster unlocks the back of his truck and the men with guns take a closer look.

The road curves away from the water and the signs say Calipatria, Westmoreland, El Centro. A huge cattle farm materializes on your left, black and whites shoulder to shoulder, packed for a mile in the desert sun. You think about becoming a vegetarian. At the agricultural town of Brawley, Latino farm workers in worn denim and white cowboy hats drift down dusty sidewalks and you head west, roll over the Alamo River and the New River, then you're headed north. The Coyote Mountains of the Anza-Borrego Desert are low in the western distance and a few minutes later there's the Salton Sea reasserting itself coolly on your right.

La Migra again, this time with dogs. Big German shepherds straining at chain leashes. You slow down and are waved through by a bored-looking official. As you pull away a large structure sprouts up along the desert shore, vivid against the sky. You roll into the town of Salton City to take a closer look. From a distance, it appears as if a giant egg yolk has been dropped on a Wal-Mart, which was then trimmed in saturated royal blue. Getting closer, you see a banner hanging from the building: West Shores Wild Cats. It's the high school. High school is tough enough to swallow anywhere in America. You think about what it must be like to attend this big yellow one on the sandy planes of the Salton Sea. The town runs along the shore. Roads loop crazily following no pattern. Houses are one story and solid, no trailers here. Across the highway is a rest stop. Compared to Bombay Beach, you are on the French Riviera.

You continue along the shore back toward Indio, the road bisecting palm-choked oases to the east and the Santa Rosa Mountains, their Mesozoic granite brown in the bleak distance to the west. Now the sun is at its scorching height, and you need to return to work and the world, so you glance over your right shoulder and take a last look at the Salton Sea, its isolation, its fragile beauty, its magnetic call that you already hear as you speed away, and you realize there is less of it now than when you started so you must hurry back before it's gone.

"Coriander Flowers"

Andrew Lam

Where Jalapeño Meets Star Anise

California cuisine has turned into crossroads cuisine.

My sister and I were strolling down Larkin Street in San Francisco recently when there wafted a pungent, salty aroma from an open window. I was about to name the dish but the couple walking ahead of us beat me to it. "Hmm, I smell fish sauce," said a blonde woman who looked to be in her mid-twenties. "Yup," agreed her male companion with tattoos on both arms. "With lots of pepper—and a little burnt."

We had reasons to laugh. First, he was right on the nose, so to speak. Second, when we first came to San Francisco from Vietnam more than three decades ago, my grandmother made catfish in a clay pot, and our Irish neighbors complained about "a toxic smell." Mortified, our family apologized and kept our windows closed whenever Grandma prepared some of her favorite recipes.

Many years passed. Grandma's gone. But I'm confident that, if she were still here, she would appreciate knowing that what was once considered unsavory (or even toxic) has become today's classic. In California, private culture has—like sidewalk stalls in Chinatown selling bok choy, string beans, and bitter melons—a knack for spilling into the public domain. Or put it this way: the Californian palate has shifted along with the state's demographics, where more than one in four are now immigrants. As of the 2000 census, 112 languages were spoken in the Bay Area alone. On warm summer afternoons, Nob Hill, where I live, turns into a modern tower of Babel. The languages of the world—Chinese, French, Spanish, German, Russian, Thai, Japanese, Hindi, Vietnamese, and many more I do not recognize—echo from the street, accompanied by assorted cooking aromas. Within a four-block radius from my home, I can experience Thai, Chinese, Spanish, Vietnamese, Moroccan, Indian, French, Mexican, Greek, Italian, and Japanese food—not to mention the regular fare at diners and seafood houses.

To live in California these days is to live at the crossroads of a global society and a global table. On its April 16, 2006, front page, the San Francisco Chronicle declared, "America's mean cuisine: More like it hot—from junk food to ethnic dishes, spicy flavors are the rage." Californians were among the first to give up blandness and savor the pungent lemongrass in our soup, and to develop a penchant for that tangy, burnt taste of spicy chili. It came as no surprise to Californians that Cheez-It came out with "Hot & Spicy" crackers flavored with Tabasco sauce, that Kettle Chips has "Spicy Thai" flavor, and that Stock Pot, a subsidiary of Campbell's Soup, makes Vietnamese pho beef broth. "There are 15.1 million more Hispanics living in the United States than there were ten years ago, and 3.2 million more Asians and Pacific Islanders," noted San Francisco's newspaper of record. "And the foods of those countries— longtime favorites with Californians—are now the nation's most popular."

Which is to say that whatever happens in California rarely stays in California. Especially in matters of taste.

In New York last winter, Irene Khin, chef and owner of Saffron 59, Inc., an upscale catering business, told me she always regarded California as the leading edge. "I have so many friends in California who are into wine and food," she said. "And you've got fresh vegetables and large ethnic groups—a great, great blessing."

Khin, who grew up in Burma, consults with restaurants around the world to come up with fusion dishes. To be on top of the game, to remain what many consider one of New York's top caterers, she travels time and againto California and Southeast Asiato sample new dishes and reacquaint herself with classics that might have been recently rejuvenated with new ingredients from Malaysia or Vietnam or Oaxaca.

One lives in an age of enormous options in an astounding, diverse, and fertile region, where human restlessness and fabulous alchemical commingling are increasingly becoming the norm.

California is, indeed, full of foodies. But to what degree do we take our foodiness? Consider the following an anecdotal answer.

I consider myself to be a well-traveled reporter and writer. But it turns out that my biggest hits at dinner parties are not my stories of hanging out with ex–Khmer Rouge soldiers in Cambodia in the early '90s, nor my trek to Mount Everest, nor my recent trip to Kish, Iran, where I talked with long-oppressed Iranian writers, nor my dusty camel ride into the Sahara. No, it's the afternoon I spent interviewing chef Hiroyuki Sakai of *Iron Chef* fame, sipping his Riesling, eating his delicious food, and listening to stories of his culinary exploits. Before Iron Chef became a national sensation on the Food Network channel and spawned two American versions, it was first aired in San Francisco, in Japanese with Chinese subtitles. Intended for a select ethnic audience, the show nevertheless garnered a large and diverse following, though most viewers understood neither Chinese nor Japanese. Friends and relatives in California all looked at me when I came back from Tokyo as if I had come down from Mount Sinai after having dined with God.

"Pepper"

Long before Webster's acknowledged the word, globalization had already swept over California. Latin and Anglo America came to an epic collision here, then gold made the state famous around the world, and the rest of the world rushed in and created a prototypical global village. Since then, layers upon layers of complexity—tastes, architecture, religions, animals, vegetables, fruits, stories, music, languages—have piled onto the place, making it in many ways postmodern before the rest of the world struggled to enter even the modern era.

Andrea Nguyen, author of *Intro the Vietnamese Kitchen: Treasured Foodways, Modern Flavors*, an authoritative book on Vietnamese cooking, declared that "California cuisine is intrinsically ethnic."

El Cocinero Español, she noted, the first work on food in the state, was a Mexican cookbook published in 1898 by Encarnación Pinedo. Translated into English in 2005 by Dan Strehl, it is now aptly titled "Encarnación's Kitchen: Mexican Recipes from Nineteenth-Century California." Nguyen, who remembers her mother packing an orange notebook full of recipes when they were airlifted out of Saigon in 1975, says Vietnamese food is hot these days.

"In the Bay Area, you've got restaurants like the Slanted Door, Crustacean, Tamarind, and Bui leading the charge in terms of crossover restaurants."

It was not always so. For the first few years in America, my family and I were terribly homesick. At dinnertime, my mother would say, "Guavas back home are ripened this time of year back at our farm," or someone else would say, "I miss mangosteen so much," and we would shake our heads and sigh. But then a friend, newly arrived to America, gave my mother some seeds and plants. Soon, her small backyard garden was full of lemongrass, Thai basil, Vietnamese coriander and small red chilies. Soon, our homesickness was eased by the knowledge that home was coming, slowly but surely, nearer to the golden shore.

Now imagine my mother's garden spreading over a large swath of California's farmland. Southeast Asian farmers are growing a variety of vegetables in the Central Valley and trucking them to markets all over the state. Hmong, Filipino, Thai, Cambodian, Vietnamese, Korean, Laotian, South Asian, and Latin American farmers join the rest and sell staples like live chickens and seafood, Thai eggplants, edible amaranth, hyacinth beans, hairy gourds, oriental squash, winter melons and sugarcane. I have learned not to underestimate the power of immigrants' nostalgia. In the Golden State, it often has ways of becoming retroactive. So much longing for home re-creates it in the new landscape. On a sunny day, I'd visit the local farmers' markets, and there would be oddly familiar fragrances and sounds that, were I to close my eyes, I could imagine myself back in my hometown in that verdant, fog-filled plateau of Dalat, Vietnam.

But if California food is intrinsically ethnic, another element is just as essential: the nature of its transgression. Here, jalapeño meets star anise and is paired with a dry, smoky pinot. Or consider the avocado. Though not served in Japanese restaurants in Japan, it is as pertinent to Japanese cuisine in California as sunny skies are to the myth of California living.

"Foodies are very curious about exotic ingredients," says Andrea Nguyen. "They're more open to venturing into Asian markets to get the 'authentic' ingredients. They're wanting to explore jujubes, mangosteens, green papaya. Ethnic markets, particularly chains like 99 Ranch and Mi Pueblo, are leading the effort to make things easier for everyone. They offer a wide variety of products. But check the aisle carefully—there are often Hispanic ingredients, too, at Asian markets, like tortillas."

Take the sign that hangs on the Sun Hop Fat 1 Supermarket on East 12th Street, a few blocks south of Lake Merritt in Oakland. It says, "American-Mexican-Chinese-Vietnamese-Thailand-Cambodia-Laos-Filipino-Oriental Food." Some might see it as evidence of diversity gone bad, a multicultural mess—that is, too much mixing makes things unpalatable, all the colors blended inevitably produce an uncomely brown. I see all those hyphens as bridges and crossroads that seek to marry far-flung ideas, tastes, and styles. Creativity is fertile when nourished in the loam of cultural diversity and cultivated with openness and a disposition for experimentation. With food, it results in an explosion of tasty concoctions. Consider some of today's daring experiments: the tofu burrito, hummus guacamole, spring rolls with a salsa dipping sauce, lamb in tamarind sauce, the lemongrass martini, a wasabi Bloody Mary, crab cakes in mango sauce, french fries dipped in mint and cilantro chutney. The variety is endless.

"Star Anise"

ANDREW

LAM

In my lifetime here I have felt the pressure to move toward some generic, standardized melting-pot center deflate—transpose, in fact, to something quite its opposite, as the demography shifts toward a society in which there's no discernible majority, no clear single center. Instead, the story I often see is one where one crosses, by various degrees, from ethnic to cosmopolitan, by traversing those various hyphens that hang over the Hop Fat supermarket. How much are food and cooking part of my California lifestyle?

I didn't really know the answer until I spent a week at a retreat in Bali last October, fasting. For six days straight I practiced yoga and ate nothing. It was supposed to be a spiritual experience. But it was tough going, with only a few fruit drinks as my meals.

Hunger, they say, is a good cook. Each night I tossed and turned and had strangely vivid dreams. Practically all of them were about cooking and eating. I seared scallops and fried prawns and tossed arugula salads and shaved Asiago cheese. I would wake each morning slightly disappointed at failing in my spiritual quest.

But then near the end of my fast, I had a dream so lucid and real it felt as if I were not dreaming at all: I was back in California, shopping at a local market. I could smell fresh basil. I could touch the heirloom tomatoes. Then I made this dish that I had never made before, a Vietnamese beef stew with a French influence—in which fish sauce and red wine are mixed, and spiced with cinnamon, ginger, and star anise. My friends gathered around a table, waiting for me to serve it. Laughter and cheers ring in the air and there is the clinking of glasses in a shared blessing. I remember thinking, on a very empty stomach: it can't get more divine than that.

"Toung Duc Me Khoc"

Aimee Phan

Little Saigon

During my second year at UCLA, I went through the typical sophomore slump. My roommate and I weren't speaking, my classes—gen ed requirements—frustrated me, and I had, inexplicably, regrettably signed up for an internship with the Rosie O'Donnell Show for its February sweeps run at the Warner Brothers Studios in Burbank. It was a brief flirtation to determine if I wanted to work in the entertainment industry. The unpaid internship was thankless slave labor where I endured a forty-five minute commute to sit in a windowless room and answer phones, while the rest of the staff got to hang out in the studio and watch the taping. Two days into the internship, I realized this business was not for me, but I had already committed to the four weeks of work. In stop-and-go traffic on the 134 freeway, I tried to talk myself down from impending panic attacks. The only thing that seemed to calm me down was a Vietnamese radio station I found while flipping stations, that was broadcasting from Little Saigon in Orange County. The weak reception crowed with static, but I didn't care. Hearing these familiar voices, even though I could barely translate their words, soothed my nerves. I could pretend, for at least a little while, that I was fine.

My roommates and friends couldn't understand my homesickness, because unlike them, my hometown of Irvine was only an hour away. To many of my classmates who hailed from the Bay Area or out of state, I hadn't really gone away to school at all. Yet I acutely felt the distance. Los Angeles did not feel like home as it did for seemingly everyone else around me. I was too shy to drink, too self-conscious to join a sorority. Instead of staying on campus during the weekends, I asked my parents to pick me up and bring me home. They were only too happy to oblige after hearing my weepy, anxious voice during our evening phone calls. Better that I was around them instead of alone in my dorm room.

On our drive home to Irvine, my father would suggest we stop in Little Saigon for a bowl of pho. It didn't matter what time of day it was or if he'd already eaten. He'd find an excuse to stop because he had faith in my favorite comfort food. We always went to the same noodle restaurant, the one we'd been going to since I was a little girl. I always got the same combination: rare steak, no onions, no cilantro. While I ate, he sipped on a Vietnamese iced coffee: a French dark roasted coffee with sweetened condensed milk. Afterward, we walked through the Asian Garden Mall, the flashy, commercial epicenter of Little Saigon, where older men read newspapers in the food court, couples flirted with each other around the fountains, and parents roamed the storefronts, picking up trinkets and music CDs, occasionally shouting at their children to stay close by. Within this hour-long combination of noodle soup and strolling, I experienced the familiar peace the Vietnamese station had provided during those traffic jams on I-134. My father brought me home to my mother and brother fully refreshed. My parents must have thought this Little Saigon medicine terribly ironic: their American-born daughter who could hardly speak Vietnamese, who used to request meatloaf or pasta for dinner while growing up. I needed their ethnic enclave more than they did.

That is probably not true. I understand now that my solace in Little Saigon, an area I didn't even grow up in, is near identical to my parents' need for it when they first arrived in this country. Unlike most of the Vietnamese refugees in America, my parents arrived before the Fall of Saigon. My mother was a graduate student at the University of Kentucky and my father worked as a dishwasher in Columbia, Missouri. After the Communists seized control of the country in April 1975, my parents realized there was no return home for them. My mother found a job in Orange County as a social worker, where she would help facilitate the immigration of Vietnamese refugees stationed in Camp Pendleton.

The refugees assigned to Pendleton ended up winning the location lottery. When the American government accepted thousands of Vietnamese refugees into the country, they were pretty deliberate about where—and how many—should go. In order to facilitate their assimilation (they learned their lesson with the Cuban immigration wave: not another Miami!), the government threaded the new refugees through every geographic fiber of the country—those that were willing, of course. That's why you will meet the occasional Vietnamese from Oklahoma and wonder how the hell he got there. But for all the government's efforts, the Vietnamese are a chatty bunch. After letter exchanges and phone call testimonies, many managed to gravitate to the part of the country that reminded them most of their sunny, coastal home: Southern California.

You can google most of these facts, but to be brief about it: Little Saigon originated on Bolsa Avenue as a small strip of grocery stores and restaurants in an economically depressed area of the city of Westminster. These businesses flourished as more Vietnamese got wind of the new places to buy Asian vegetables and go out for a decent plate of *banh cuon*. As more Vietnamese and Vietnamese-Chinese refugees relocated to the area and opened businesses, the community spread to Garden Grove, Fountain Valley, Santa Ana, and the surrounding areas. My brother and I would know instantly when we arrived in Little Saigon—the Vietnamese language signs, the trademark red-roof buildings, the colorful posters for the Vietnamese variety show *Paris By Night*. How could we not? We were there nearly every day.

Despite my parents' loyalty to the area, we never lived there. By the time my younger brother was born, my parents had bought a house in the master-planned community of Irvine, a harbinger of what was to come for southern Orange County. The two areas, though both thoroughly suburban, couldn't feel more different. While Irvine thrived on preciousness and uniformity, down to the number of trees on each grassy street divider and the matching wooden storefront signs in the shopping centers, Little Saigon unquestionably felt more urban, cluttered with billboards, box stores and strip malls of all sizes. While I hardly saw anyone walking around in Irvine, except in the manicured parks, the streets in Little Saigon bustled with chatty pedestrians toting sun umbrellas, pink plastic bags full of greasy barbecued pork and tiny grocery carts.

While this confused my brother and me (the twenty-minute freeway commute could balloon into an hour in heavy traffic), my parents seemed content co-existing between these two worlds. Irvine was a dream community for any worried parent: it is consistently voted one of the safest cities in America. To own a home there was the pinnacle of their American dream. But while they liked the house and the parks and the virtual absence of crime, they did not like the expensive mainstream grocery stores, the fast food restaurants, or the fact that they were the only Vietnamese people in our very white neighborhood. So they could sleep quite soundly in their beds in Irvine; once they woke up and felt hungry, it was time to pile into our Camry and drive to Bolsa. My parents conducted all their errands in Little Saigon, from our grocery shopping to optometrist and dental visits to our occasional dinners out. They never seemed happier and more at ease than when they were in Little Saigon because no one ever looked twice at them or blinked at their accents or asked them to repeat the question. No one ever wondered if they belonged. For my parents, who would be separated from their family for years, this inclusion became essential and easily worth the gas money to visit.

Every return to Southern California must include a stop in Little Saigon, and my requisite, but always genuine wonder at how the area continues to grow and thrive. While I always knew the Vietnamese American community in Southern California could be quite mighty, I never would have guessed that Little Saigon would continue to spread throughout Orange County. Once the only Vietnamese in the neighborhood, my parents now have an Asian shopping mall five minutes away from their house. Though they still claim the groceries are too expensive at the Ranch 99 and that the broth at the pho restaurant down the street is subpar, I know they are pleased to have such conveniences nearby.

The community's influence is not restricted to cuisine. With anti-Communist sentiment still very strong among the Vietnamese, Little Saigon has become a political lightning rod for the already conservative Orange County. The Asian Garden Plaza is a popular Republican campaign stop for political candidates, most famously presidential nominee John McCain, who notoriously referred to his Communist captors as "gooks" in the national media. The ensuing debate further highlighted the political differences between the conservative older generation and their more liberal children. Vietnamese-American politicians now occupy public offices, with the first Vietnamese-American elected to the state legislature in 2004. Little Saigon boasts several Vietnamese language newspapers, television and radio stations, which offer varied opinions on local, national and global events. The community has also emerged as the center of the Vietnamese pop music industry, outpacing Vietnam itself. Every year, the Vietnamese student associations at the local universities and colleges organize the Tet Festival, which offers cultural shows, carnival rides, and local street food to thousands of attendees.

I try to follow the community's developments, as fast as they come, since Little Saigon is a major facet in my fiction writing. This wasn't a setting I ever thought to use when I started writing fiction. It took moving out of state to Iowa for graduate school for me to realize how perfect, how essential, the community was to my characters and subject. It doesn't even seem fair to relegate Little Saigon to a setting, given its significance in my work. Little Saigon has become as important as any major character in my short stories or novel.

My brother and I both have careers that have taken us out of Orange County. I think my parents always secretly hoped we would return, and now that they are getting older, they are afraid of another forced relocation, though it's been over thirty-five years since their last move. My father commonly expresses this anxiety. He knows the streets and freeways between Irvine and Little Saigon by heart. He complains that he is too old to try to learn a new route. Considering how important Little Saigon has been to me during the lost periods in my life, knowing how much of it I want to show to my own daughter, I can't bear the thought of going against his wish, no matter how increasingly unpractical it becomes. I remember my grandfather in the last years of his life, crying every time he moved from one daughter's home to another, because the family was sharing the responsibility of caring for him during his Alzheimer's. It didn't matter if he was leaving a condo in Lakewood or a small house in Lubbock, Texas. He was being uprooted again, when he'd never had time to adjust from his first unwilling departure—out of Vietnam. My grandfather never recovered from leaving Vietnam. After so many years making Orange County his home, my father shouldn't have to suffer the same fate.

"That Way to Safety"

Matt Shears

I have a conflicted relationship with California. Most native Midwesterners do. Even those who choose to reside here—and there are many—do so by distancing themselves, both geographically and psychologically, from their own foundations. Some want to do this, of course, and certainly one could make the same claim about moving anywhere—Ohio even—from anywhere else. Of the fifty states, however, California boasts an almost mythic status. Rightly or wrongly, American history (and by that I mean U.S. history) has always been told from right to left and, anachronistically or not, California often seems the transcendent signifier of this westward expansion. Many California writers have pointed out that this is precisely because the state exists outside the barbed-wire fence of Manifest Destiny. It developed not in accord with the ethos of a westward-looking European Protestantism, but through a complex mix of unincorporated peoples and cultures that have more to do with "New Spain," Spanish speaking, Catholic, Native American, mestizo— than with "New England." It's Melville's placid Pacific, versus the turgidity of the Atlantic and all it signifies.

While I appreciate this view, it, like the dream of the West, is a romance. Cortez was no more a gentleman than Custer, and the Spanish conquest of Old Mexico was surely as brutal as anything Andrew Jackson cooked up.

Despite this, when viewed from afar, the idea of California glitters with stardust, and its loci of freedom—free thought, free action, free speech, free love—offer a real sense of possibility. Or perpetually threaten the status quo. Whatever the idea of California does to non-Californians, the state is nothing if not dynamic. I'm reminded of a saying from my childhood, a prevalent sentiment, at least within the circles I traveled. It goes something like this: When they were making the United States, they tipped the country on its side to corral all the freaks in one area. That area? Yup. You guessed it. Being one of those freaks myself, I am now less inclined to see the humor in the statement, but I think it is instructive to note that similar dicta about other western states—Idaho, say, or Nevada—just don't have the same resale value. California is an otherworldly place, an ethereal presence, a thing in itself, pure and simple. Or so it seemed to a guy from "flyover country."

But enough about the imaginary. The Midwestern work ethic in me demands that I get down to business. Here's the deal: my partner loves In-N-Out burgers. She announced this to a crowd of people in an apartment in Iowa City, Iowa during the frigid winter of 2001. I had never heard of In-N-Out Burgers but I was familiar with the general concept of the hamburger 'n' fries and have been known to partake from time to time. The room was full of beefy beef experts; hamburger theorists and hamburger empiricists, hamburger grillers, broilers, orderers and possibly even hamburger thieves. Clearly my partner had been called to arms, and calmly stated that In-N-Out burgers were the best burgers around. Fightin' words. Luckily for her, another native Californian backed up her claim: fresh, cheap, delicious—the lovechild McDonald's wished it could have had. The talk went on for awhile, but it was already clear to me that, at least on this day, the Midwest had lost yet another battle it really believed it should have won: the battle for a Beef Patty of Truth covered by a generous slice of melted Americana.

Four years later or so, I was finally able to test out my partner's brazen claim. I had to admit: she had a strong case. But this isn't just about burgers. It's also about that other time-honored Americanism: driving an automobile. To the best of my knowledge, no other cross-section of the population loves driving quite so much as Midwesterners. Both hamburgers and cars perhaps hearken to idealized images of post-war America—the good old days of opulence, complacency, and an unimaginable homogeneity. But America's relationship with its cars is perhaps even more complicated than my relationship with California. Luckily, California is a big, long state, and two of its major arteries travel right up through the San Joaquin Valley. I've driven the length of the state many times, and I've gotten pretty familiar with both its roads and its hamburgers. The drive can be beautiful, idyllic even; vast open stretches that speed through rolling hills. The Central Valley is a hotter, sunnier simulacrum of the bucolic landscapes of my youth. I love to drive and my partner loves to find In-N-Out Burgers, so there are a few stops on the I-5 that pique our joint interest. One in particular stands out: Kettleman City.

⁂

There are a lot of places one could write about when writing about California, micro-histories galore, untold tales among the major culture-shaping events of history, perhaps the reasons California lends itself so well to myth-making. I could tell you about why I enjoy living in Oakland, what is special about the consciousness of Berkeley, what can be magical about crossing the Bay Bridge into San Francisco proper, what is beautiful about the natural preserves surrounding the Bay Area. Kettleman City, though, is a different story.

Immense tracts of California are absolutely invisible; awash in a silence composed and comprised by a chorus of the voiceless. And Kettleman City is truly an invisible city, an invisible, silent city. I should clarify. Everybody's been there or been by there, but few people have gone further into Kettleman City than the Regular Unleaded pump at one of the gas stations, or the cash register of one of the fast food joints,, and few people have stayed longer than the time it takes to consider adding onions (fresh, by the way) to their burger magnifique. So it shouldn't come as a huge surprise that federal and state governments haven't paid much attention to the place. But for us, Kettleman City was a mecca of sorts. Anytime we'd make the drive from Oakland to Orange County to see my partner's family, we'd try to hold off eating and refueling until Kettleman City, three hours away. We would cheer as we crested those rolling Kettleman Hills and saw the sign for our beacon—the In-N-Out up ahead. We even planned our three-month-old daughter's first long car ride around a stop in Kettleman City. I can still remember, as a clueless new dad, changing a diaper in the backseat of the Camry in the In-N-Out parking lot. Good times.

I must confess: I don't think about Kettleman City all the time. I don't think many people do. But when I heard a story recently concerning malnutrition in Kettleman City, my ears perked up. Kettleman City, rest stop, population 2,000 or so, newsworthy? Referenced on *Morning Edition*? The news there was news to me: no sidewalks, no streetlights, no grocery store, no fresh food. How couldn't I have noticed? I mean, I don't require much as rest stops go, but I'd like to think I'm cognizant enough of my surroundings to observe significant amendments to my expectations, however bourgeois, even if they make their way into my consciousness by way of absence. "Fast food culture," said the story—that I had observed—a fast food culture that locals can neither avoid nor escape. California's Central Valley is often talked about as the breadbasket of the country (California: 2 Iowa: 0) and the story claimed that locals didn't even have the opportunity to partake of the fruits of their own labor. While I found the slant on childhood obesity to be a compelling one, I also began to wonder about other socioeconomic factors.

Less than four miles away from Kettleman City is a sixteen-hundred-acre land-fill (five hundred acres of which are designated Class I and accept hazardous waste) run by Chemical Waste Management. They've been running the hazardous waste landfill since the late '70s, the only landfill in the state, in fact, that accepts PCB's—polychlorinated biphenyls—carcinogenic compounds outlawed by the U.S. govern-ment around the same time Chemical Waste Management broke ground just outside Kettleman City. After the local oil wells dried up in the '50s, the area converted to a primarily agricultural zone, and around 70% of the population is now Latino. A significant portion of the population speaks Spanish exclusively, and the area has an unemployment rate of somewhere around 25%.

While always disappointing to consider, it is no secret that hazardous waste dumps don't normally break ground amid the mansions of the affluent. And despite the fact that there was a pollution protest held in Kettleman City recently, there is no hard evidence anywhere that Chemical Waste Management is poisoning the resi-dents of the area. Despite that fact, corroborated by the Environmental Protection Agency Scorecard, the Pollution Information site lists King's County, where Kettle-man City is located, in the top ten percent of dirtiest counties nationwide regarding industrial contaminants. The site lists Chemical Waste Management as releasing 11.6 million pounds in 2002 alone. This "Pollutant Report Card" also lists King's County in the bottom ten percent of counties nationwide regarding agricultural contaminants. Reports of asthma and other respiratory diseases are common, despite the fact that research suggests winds in the area blow from north to south. That is to say, Kettleman City is not directly downwind of Chemical Waste Management.

But something's missing from the picture. Residents have long complained about high cancer rates in the area and, more recently, a rash of birth defects has beset the town. In the past year and a half, five children have been born with birth defects—that's roughly thirty percent of reported births in the area. Three of those children have died.

Chance? Take a look at this, referenced from a 1993 *New York Times* article:

A growing body of evidence that minorities suffer the most from pollution and benefit the least from cleanup programs is transforming environmental politics.

Roberto Suro's article continues:

> "We are the real endangered species in America, people of color," said Susana Almanza, a leader of a community protest in Austin, Tex., that succeeded last fall in forcing the closing of a gasoline terminal in a black and Hispanic residential area. "We're the ones who are dying with the cancer clusters and the birth defects because of the air we breathe."

The article was written, in part, to introduce what it calls "the environmental justice movement and, sadly, could easily have been written about Kettleman City in the present day. Environmental groups call this situation environmental racism, and only through Kettleman City's invisibility (or our own inability to see it) could we possibly think otherwise.

*

I'll admit it: I like cows. I think they are magnificent creatures, especially up close. I always feel tremendously guilty when I really think about them, the lives they lead in captivity, their slaughter, their conversion into foodstuffs. In my fits of conscience I become a vegetarian and am all the happier for it. Still, I love watching cows as I drive the interstates because they make me think of my home and my youth. I've got a friend who likes them even more than I do: his name is Rick North. He spent a lot of time working with the American Cancer Society and now works as an activist, educator and lobbyist for hormone-free cow's milk. That label on the milk you buy—rBGH-free? That was part of his doing. It stands for recombinant bovine growth hormone, and it's been linked with cancer. When I see a hill full of cows, I think about his battles with that super-chemical company Monsanto, and I think about how his work is often undone by their immense network of invested supporters. Interestingly, Monsanto took over the production of PCB's—the chemicals that designate the Kettleman Hills landfill a hazardous waste site—in 1929, and produced them until they were outlawed.

I had realized when we first stopped in Kettleman City, several years ago now, that the bucolic landscape I watched—and yearned for, really—was more complicated than its image suggested. The bucolic landscape is always far away, and it is only comforting because it is in the distance. I grew up realizing the rural areas around me experienced life and poverty in a different way, but since then I've been in transit.

When you're driving, no matter how much you enjoy it, everything tends to blur. It's like you're living an updated version of Zeno's Paradox, both moving and not moving at the same time. But you also start to focus solely on the road. At some point, the landscape disappears and you simply experience duration as duration. Indeed, time stops (part of Zeno's point, perhaps) and it only seems to commence once you step out of the vehicle.

Time stopped for my partner and me when we suddenly glimpsed the invisible parts of Kettleman City: the invisible people, the invisible government, the invisible powers-that-be, the invisible disease, the invisible reach of capital, the invisible landscape, the invisible lives, the invisible deaths. As we listened to the radio report on Kettleman City, we understood these particular problems to be an example of the price migrant and immigrant labor pays for the chance to work. And yet we also understood them to be larger than one state could contain. We saw, in an instant, the invisible disenfranchised. It was like we were always looking out the wrong window, or scoping across the fields for that In-N-Out sign in the distance. Finally, we were there.

Kate Gale

Zaca Lake

Ask people in what is now known as "*Sideways* Country," because of the movie *Sideways*, which forever ruined the Santa Ynez Wine Country, or enhanced it, depending on your perspective, ask those people where Zaca Lake is, and most of them will just shrug. It's in Los Olivos, the wine country of the Central Coast, tucked away off Zaca Station Road, which you reach by coming up the 101 from Santa Barbara. It's right after Buellton, if you're coming north.

We discovered Zaca Lake on Memorial Day weekend twelve years ago. We planned to go the Sequoias but the campground was snowed in. We started through our California book of things to do and found a lake north of Santa Barbara. We called; they had an opening at a cabin, and we have been going there ever since. That's how things happen in California. Natural disaster equals new opportunity.

Those first few years were magical. George and Rose ran the place. We cooked in the communal kitchen. The restaurant had just been closed and the kitchen was huge and had everything. We worked around whoever else was there, usually a yoga group which consisted of one male yoga leader with flowing grey hair and great posture, and twenty female followers. We taught our children to sail, canoe, kayak, hike. There was no trouble for them to get into except poison oak. All of them were excellent swimmers and the lake, a thick murky green, took about twenty minutes to swim from shore to shore. I have swum across it in February when I thought my heart was going to leap out of my body, and I have swum across it so many times in August that my family thought I would never come out for dinner. In the middle of the lake, you are at the middle of a huge bowl of green, the mountains up around you on all sides, and you at the bottom of the bowl. There are water rushes around the edges and water birds nesting with their young.

A little history. The entire Zaca Lake area was peopled by the Chumash Indians, whose territory went from Malibu to Paso Robles and inland to the edge of the San Joaquin Valley. The Chumash were a rich tribe numbering tens of thousands. As with all California tribes, the Spanish missions enslaved and decimated them in the 1700s and 1800s. Zaca Lake had been a sacred center and school for the Chumash people for thousands of years and the Chumash still say that the energy of Zaca Lake is unique. Zaca Lake is California's largest naturally occurring lake. It is forty-sex feet at its deepest. There's a myth that the lake is bottomless, due to a sinkhole that seems impossible to measure for depth. The surrounding mountains include Zaca Peak, Wild Horse Mountain and Lookout Mountain.

The lake is owned as a non-profit and is available for camping or cabin rentals, individually or as a group. Over the years of our going to Zaca Lake, the place has gradually changed. The dining room, which was slowly sliding into the lake, has been fixed. Now, since the kitchen is closed, it is irrelevant because you can't eat there. One of the great joys of Zaca was cooking in the kitchen, then sitting at the tables by the lake, watching the fish come up through the rushes and the moon rise while you eat dinner. But that has been closed.

The boats, canoes, and sailboats have disappeared too. All of the family cabins and the yurt have tripled in price so now we cannot afford to stay there. The one cabin had its own kitchen and the other had a bedroom for kids and one for the adults. Now, when we go, our entire family huddles into one small cabin. We have the teenagers on sleeping bags on the floor and all of us in the same room. We're like families in the Middle Ages.

Because fewer people come to Zaca, the wildlife is much more intrusive. On our last visit, the raccoons came right up to our table during dinner and sat down to have food with us. I'm half kidding. They sat on the floor next to the table. I expect at our next visit they'll be in the cabin. All our food had to be cooked over a tiny barbecue grill. Making coffee wasn't easy. With a cooler and the tiny grill, it was like camping very expensively in a cabin.

You're asking why we still go. Because the lake is still there in all its loveliness, murky green with all that sky and trees and mountain held in its face. We see bear. I saw a baby bear ten feet away from me. (I didn't get any closer.) We see turkey, raccoons, squirrels and there is a pair of bald eagles. The turkeys were released in the area to be hunted but have gone wild and now stalk about, hunted by the bear. We take one day to go wine tasting, right out the gate and we are at Zaca Mesa Winery, where people don't even know the lake is there.

On July 4, 2007, we were wakened by helicopters flying over Zaca Lake to collect water. The Zaca Lake fire had begun, and we were evacuated. We moved up to Pismo and watched fireworks from there while the fire got going. The fire burned 240,000 acres making it the second largest fire in California's recorded history. NASA took pictures of the fire from space. The fire was not declared controlled until October 29, 2007. We found Zaca because of one act of nature and had to escape it because of another.

It's a secret place, very strange for California. The people who come there admit that it's falling apart, that the magic of the place is something you can't hold or describe. It may be mythic; it may be that those of us who love Zaca Lake, like the Chumash, see the sacred in a place where wild animals will still look at you like you're not a stranger, but a guest. California's all about inventing your own myth. It may be falling apart, like everything in California is, but some of us stay here because of the sky and the water and the unbearable light.

"Hollywoodland Sign"

Patt Morrison

THE PICTURES-PERFECT CITY

Why here?

Why did the distant burg of Los Angeles become to the movies what Mesopotamia and Athens were to ancient civilizations?

Why not Long Island, where the earliest filmmakers trespassed onto plutocrats' lawns and shot hurried footage until they were chased off?

Why not Flagstaff, where Cecil B. DeMille was originally headed when he left the East Coast to make a western?

Why not Paris, where filmmaking was regarded as an art in the creative pantheon of arts, not as a commodity?

Because we're a perfect match, the both of us, the city and "the industry." Quick-change artists on the make, inventive, rootless, not wedded to history—not even dating it.

L.A. is a soufflé place, built on sunshine and hot air, equal parts imagination and aspiration. Film is by nature illusory, the moment vanishing even as the eye acknowledges it, still images miming motion, fantasy miming reality. When the movies came west, the transient carnival mood of L.A. was already established, a slapdash build-up and tear-down city, cheerfully doting on its fake Venice canals, its copycat Asian temples. For years, remnants of the Babylon set of *Intolerance* crumbled amiably near Sunset Boulevard as ever-newer incarnations of six-cylinder chariots thundered by.

All this under the rotisserie glow of sunlight as full and obliging as if gaffers had set it all up for the next shot. The movies became California's second Gold Rush, and the richest vein was to be found in a dry little settlement named Hollywood.

Why not "Long Island, the Entertainment Capital of the World?" Because the arm of film patent attorneys didn't reach across the Rockies to snag the scofflaws. Why not Flagstaff? Because it happened to be snowing the day DeMille arrived, which made it "no good for our purpose," he telegrammed, and promptly climbed back on the train to L.A. And why not France? Because in the struggle for the soul of film, the Lumiere brothers lost to the Warner brothers.

So Hollywood became the geographic shorthand for the entire entertainment industry, though its footprint reaches from George Lucas's fantasy factory in Marin County to the Death Valley vistas of *Greed*, and every point of latitude or longitude that could conceivably be "on location." And although Los Angeles has prospered in making everything from jets to blue jeans, "the industry" means only one: film and TV and its numberless incarnations.

"L.A." to most of the millions of Angelenos means the whole great sprawling populated plain; it means any of dozens of towns where the only contact most residents have with movies is that they sometimes watch them. Hollywood has blithely appropriated all of Los Angeles as its terrain, their "L.A." a company town. The late former Mayor Sam Yorty said that once, on his extensive world travels talking up the virtues of the city to foreign industrialists and heads of state, one of them ruminated aloud to him: "Los Angeles . . . Los Angeles . . . is that anywhere near Hollywood?"

For fans who still step off the tour bus expecting to see this generation's Garbo or Gable awaiting them, the matrix of glamour is Grauman's Chinese, or maybe Hollywood and Vine, both on the boulevard where ground glass was mixed into the asphalt so the roadway glitters at night.

For the hard-nosed Angelenos who take Hollywood's paycheck, the epicenter was for years Beverly Boulevard and La Cienega. Thirty miles in any direction from there was "the studio zone." Beyond that was the rest of the world, and location shoots and per diems, and mileage, and the "sticks" and "hicks" of *Variety* headlines. It may still be L.A., but it is absorbed in other matters, other businesses. It is why studio heads of the 1930s shuttled film canisters to places like Riverside and Santa Barbara, where "real" audiences could preview them and scribble Everyman suggestions and reactions that shaped the final film.

Within that magic circle, Hollywood and L.A. are often one population commuting blithely between the real and the not-real. The fluorescent signs with a cryptic word or two, and an arrow pointing cast and crew to some day's location shoot, hang like paper fruit from street lamps and electric poles. The city itself is one vast set, recognizable even in silent black-and-white two-reelers. Laurel and Hardy still haul a piano up steps that locals traverse every day. The chameleon dress-extra, City Hall, plays the Vatican and Congress, and gets zapped by Martian rays. The heap of boulders known as Vasquez Rocks is the made-to-order set for the Neolithic Flint-stones and the *Star Trek* cast.

The spectacular car crash you can see from the freeway—is it the real thing or a staged stunt? One Easter Monday, a twenty-some-foot-long prop alligator lay on a flatbed truck near Echo Park Lake, a fake human hand poking out of its jaws. Around the curve, six young men carried a pink coffin up a set of church steps—a real girl, dead in gang crossfire. In much the same fashion, Californians have seen the familiar face on television with the identifier "Governor Ronald Reagan" or "Governor Arnold Schwarzenegger," and wondered afresh: Is it a movie, or life?

The forebears of today's actors showed up with their battered baggage to find boardinghouse notices reading "no dogs or actors." The city's peerage—its Midwest millionaires, their clubs and neighborhoods—likewise snubbed the newcomers. It is the triumph of the former lumberjacks and acrobats and shop girls and waitress-es that the medium of film elevated them—however briefly or enduringly—to the world's aristocrats.

The monarchs of the movie palaces delivered immediate intimacy—the faces and gestures of Charlie and Fatty and Rudolph and Lillian and Dorothy were almost as well known to fans as their own.

THE NEW PACESETTERS

So it was that within the enchanted radius of "the studio zone," there now lived and worked a population of suddenly rich actors and writers and producers and ward-robe and set and makeup experts who remade the world's manners and attitudes. The movies, and TV—film's Mordred, its ambitious son—taught us a new vocabulary. We still assemble conversations from scraps and bits of script: "They're heeeeere . . . We're not in Kansas anymore . . . Here's looking at you, kid . . . I made him an offer he couldn't refuse . . . You talkin' to me?"

It was they, unschooled, sometimes semiliterate and slovenly spoken, who taught the twentieth century its etiquette, its notions of class and courtship. Browned skin once bespoke manual labor and sweat—until Doug Fairbanks swaggered about in a suntan and a smile, and made bronze the gold standard of the leisure glass. Hefty bod-ies and substantial meat-and-potatoes meals epitomized wealth and station—until the wraithlike Garbo slid narrowly on screen, and, off screen, ate salads and juices with her health-food guru, Gayelord Hauser. Humphrey Bogart's snarl, Joan Crawford's shoulder pads, John Travolta's strut—all envied and copied and reconfigured.

Even reality bent its knee to the power of the medium that President Woodrow Wilson marveled was "like writing history with lightning." The bona-fide frontier lawman Wyatt Earp was buddies with the movie cowboy William S. Hart. Boxing champ Max Baer costarred with Abbott and Costello. Audie Murphy, the most decorated soldier in World War II, was recruited by Hollywood to play hero soldiers like himself, but it was the Duke, John Wayne, playing cowboy, lover, Mongol prince, patriot, all in one film career, who was more authentic-seeming than the real thing. Life is always just more in the movies—skies are bluer or bleaker, sex is sexier, grit is grittier, guns and breasts are bigger. It takes a Golden State metaphor to assess movies as writer Wallace Stegner sized up California: "Like America, only more so."

Patt Morrison

Our True Heartthrob

Dearly beloved, repeat these words:

"I, Los Angeles, take thee, the internal combustion engine . . . for better or worse, for richer or poorer, in sickness and in health. . . ."

What a long, blissful marriage it's been. We're still as much in love as we were at the beginning: from the two o'clock hour one May morning in 1897, when the city's first car hit the downtown streets, to the tomorrow when the latest one rolls off the dealer's lot, bright as a bride.

This marriage has endured because we need each other. And we'll do just about anything to make our partner happy. Dairies or wedding chapels, just drive on through. Los Angeles' grandest Art Deco department store—Bullocks Wilshire—was designed not for the shopper on foot but, with its elaborate porte-cochere and parking lot, for the shopper on four wheels. Car sale ads, page upon lavish page, read like a matchmaker's come-ons; this one's a "cherry." That one's a "cream puff."

A man would rather acknowledge that his kids are ugly than admit that he's a bad driver, but you know what? Some of the offspring of this union really are ugly. Carjackings, drive-by shootings. Smog. And traffic. "The traffic question has become a problem," *The Times* admonished. The City Council "must keep the automobiles moving." This was 1910. Four years later, when fuel hit nineteen cents a gallon, the city had convened a Municipal Commission on the Gas Shortage.

Every matrimonial ride hits a few bumps, and we've had ours—little flings with red cars and yellow cars, the RTD and the MTA. We've messed around with Metrolink on the side. We've even dabbled in polygamy, some of us, taking a second and even third vehicle—an SUV, a truck, maybe an RV.

But nothing has come between us for long. Our heart belongs to horsepower.

Earthquakes have shaken this place but nothing has shaped it like our mad automobile love.

Our neighborhoods, our suburbs, are crafted around the means for getting out. The freeways, the great concrete rivers of freeways, the super-elevated sacred monsters, are christened with names, not only numbers. The four-level interchange, graceful as an ice skater's twirl, stars on its own postcards. In 1938, we built a Spanish colonial gas station in Brentwood, with a tower where a man, James Poe, lived and wrote an Oscar-winning screenplay, *Around the World in 80 Days*. Now it's a cultural historical landmark, and not because of the screenplay.

There's valet parking at the gym, the lingerie shop, the post office. And acres and miles and palaces of parking. All those original millions meant to build the Walt Disney Concert Hall were spent just on the parking garage.

The car is our legs. For all our love of lean and trim and fit, the rubber that meets our road is more often radials than running shoes.

The car populates our urban lore: Yes, a Beverly Hills woman really did get buried sitting in her red Ferrari. Yes, the illegally parked car of a past mayor, Tom Bradley, was once towed away—by the airport police who worked for him. And yes, anyplace in L.A. is only twenty minutes' drive from anyplace else.

The car is belief, and it is art. Each year, at the Blessing of the Cars, an ordained priest of the Holy Catholic and Apostolic Church flicks a sprinkle of holy water on the diamond-flake finish of a succession of pimped-out classics, hot rods and low riders. The lurid goings-on in Ed Kienholz's *Back Seat Dodge '38* nearly got it banned from the county museum forty years ago; only when no children were nearby would the guards open the car's back doors to reveal what was going on inside—something every teenager already knew about anyway.

The car gets more film work than most actors on the SAG roster. The plot of *Sunset Boulevard* begins with a hot car and an empty garage. Its crushing moment is that it isn't Norma Desmond the movie studios want, but her leopard-upholstered Isotta Fraschini. James Dean's death would not haunt us if he'd been a pedestrian hit by a Porsche, instead of the driver behind the wheel of one.

It is our id and our superego. We will do without a job. We can do without a home. But not without a car.

It gives us control. We may be the minimum-wage drudge, the weenie gofer, but assume the steering-wheel position and, like a superhero transformed, we are master and commander, the equal of anyone else on the road, limited only by SigAlerts and the size of the gas tank.

It gives us pleasure. Maria, in Joan Didion's novel *Play It as It Lays*, remakes the *Odyssey* in L.A. fashion. She squares the circle when she presses the accelerator and orbits the incantatory, mesmerizing loop of freeways.

To drive the Pasadena Freeway is to partner your car through a three-lane waltz, a minuet of curves. Driving a freeway flowing at top speed is like playing a video game—no, it's like being inside one. The noise, the lights, the motion, fast and fluid, the joystick wheel negotiating the road ahead, put Xbox physics in your hands and at your feet.

It gives us privacy. At home, the kids are squalling. At work, the boss is yowling. But the car is in the zone. It is another room on your house. That it happens to have wheels is incidental. Get in. Shut the door. Shed your shoes. Eat. Drink. Shave. Dress. Call your mom. The comfort level is absolute.

The car is inviolate. If there is any such thing as roadway etiquette, it dictates the tenuous, mutual fiction that the windshield and windows are opaque. The deliberate non-acknowledgment, that one looks but does not see, is broken at your peril, and only in moments of peril. To provoke, to mad-dog the driver in the next lane with the insolence of eye contact, is to court confrontation.

It's called a car. Usually, it can accommodate four people easily. It travels comfortably at sixty miles per hour, on treaded rubber tires. It comes in a style and size and price to fit almost any budget. And it runs on fossil fuel and faith and myth.

Patt Morrison

Land of Reinvention

In 1510, a Spanish writer named Garci Ordonez de Montalvo published a fantasist novel called *Las Sergas de Esplandian*, about a golden island ruled by a dark-skinned Amazon queen called Califia. This book would end up giving California its name.

About a hundred years later, another Spanish writer named Miguel de Cervantes wrote a book about a character who happened to own a copy of that earlier novel—a character who was arguably the first modern Californian.

Cervantes' creation, Alonso Quijada, believed that he was not a prisoner of time and place and class but that he could reinvent himself as who he wished to be, and the man he wished to be was . . . Don Quixote de la Mancha.

Don Quixote, a Californian in spirit before any such name existed on the world's mental map. Was he an idealist or a delusionary? Does it really matter? You could ask the same question about almost every Californian, every ship-jumping, border-hopping newcomer, every small-town beauty queen with a one-way bus ticket to Hollywood, every garage-band musician and garage start-up computer geek.

To each of the multitudes of men who swarmed into California after the gold strike at Sutter's Mill, the 10,000-to-1 odds of panning himself a fortune meant only that 9,999 poor dopes would be out of luck. The one—well, that was always him.

Like the Magi, every nation, every culture, leaves some gift of itself to the world. California's is the gift of reinvention, the push to the next frontier, the break through the next boundary: the American frontier, the space frontier, the nano-frontier of science and technology, even the boundary of self. Here, we are all Eves and Adams, with no past, no class, no patterns to follow, the only limits the ones of our own making.

The celebrity is the ultimate incarnation of this ideal—the nobody who suddenly becomes everything the world desires and admires. But street by street and town by town, California is peopled with those who have done just as well. Their stories are fill-in-the-blank tales of triumph: I was born in poverty and decided that I could do better than I might have had I stayed. So I studied/worked/escaped to pursue my dream and found my way to California.

For a brief time during the Gold Rush, one in every ninety Americans was making his way to California. Like Quixote, they were idealistic or delusional, or perhaps they had run out of prospects and hope elsewhere and had nowhere else to run but to the end of the continent. The difference was this, as historian J.S. Holliday, the great chronicler of the Gold Rush, reflected to PBS:

> As nowhere else, you can fail in California. And I think the California Gold Rush taught people that failure was OK. And the reason being that everyone failed in California—everyone, every day. So failure was not a distinction, not a burden, not a mark, not a shame. Failure in Des Moines, failure in Youngstown, failure in Savannah, failure in Philadelphia, well, you'd hear, 'What's the matter with you? Your father's disappointed in you.' You don't want to fail at home. But you feel free to fail in California. The result is that people accepted failure—which is the equivalent of saying they are willing to take risks. And California has been the most risk-taking economy and society in the nation. Maybe in the world.

In California, then, there was no failure—there were only delays on the way to success. It is the single, shared, defining element of being Californian, the capacity for endless reinvention. Got something to sell? To create? To popularize? A gimmick, a diet, a school, a religion? Yourself? Welcome to California.

The young Carol Burnett was as broke as they come, living with a grandmother who pinched the toilet paper from the Hollywood movie palace where Burnett was eventually fired from her job as an usherette. She asked that her star on the Hollywood Walk of Fame be placed smack in front of that theater. And in the fashion of these things, Burnett wound up buying the Beverly Hills home built by Thomas Thorkildsen, the "Borax King" who made millions with household cleansers, which were sold on television by Ronald Reagan, who fashioned himself into an actor and then a governor and president. Thorkildsen died a pensioner.

California burst into being in the modern age, always moving at the speed of its contemporaries, the railroad, the steamship, the jet, the Internet. Its mythology is not in antiquity but in memory, inspirational and aspirational. Its Olympus is populated by gods of their own making and remaking: Charlie Chaplin, Walt Disney, John Muir, Bill Hewlett and Dave Packard, Cesar E. Chavez and Arnold Schwarzenegger.

The nation sometimes finds us risible and slightly alarming, an invert of the natural order. A barely year-old online venture called YouTube makes joint billionaires out of its twenty-something creators. And an eighty-nine-year-old billionaire mogul grapples with a paternity fight. Age is stood on its head. Grow old with dignity? Who needs to grow old at all? Plastic surgery is only a means to make the face match what the spirit wills.

Even the deep, shuddering earthquakes and vast fires that the rest of the country smirks over—a proper chastisement for our ways, surely—are the kinetic landscape's means of doing what Californians do: renewing itself, shaking out, starting over.

Californians have a natural collaborator in their perpetual rewrites of themselves: the climate. In Southern California in particular, the endless, seamless flow of seasons makes time itself seem, if not to stand still, then to dawdle its way through the calendar. Here we don't feel the tightening cycles of years as people do in other, more immoderate climates. Look outside today, tomorrow, next week, to this changeless place; there's all the time in the world to try again, fail again, try yet again.

And that book, that mischief-making book *Las Sergas de Esplandian* that put such ideas in the brain of that poor hidalgo, Alonso Quijada? In the Cervantes novel, it was plucked from among the bookshelves of Quixote's library, and in the curate's purging decision to banish from Quixote's deranged mind all the nefarious influences of imagination, *Sergas* was the first book flung out the window, destined for the bonfire.

Every burned book, said Ralph Waldo Emerson, enlightens the world. Emerson was a clear-eyed utopian. He would have liked it here.

Gordon Wheeler

The Ventana Mountains along the Big Sur Coast are a young range, jammed up only a couple of million years ago by the colliding and grinding of the Pacific and North American tectonic plates along the San Andreas Fault. Countless lesser faults splinter out from this master crack, crisscrossing each other up cliffs and down canyons out over the ocean floor, yielding a jumble of ridges and canyons and opening up fissures that snake down to the earth's hot magma core. These fissures account for the hot springs that dot the California coast, including the legendary oceanside baths at Esalen, perched on a narrow ledge where the springs bubble out of the cliff face almost touching the Pacific surf below.

You can sense some of this restless young energy as you drive along the Pacific Coast Highway toward Esalen. The cliffs are jagged, not yet settled in their own mountain bodies, like new-grown adolescents uncertain of their own sudden bulges and angles. The mountains even have their own wet dreams, heaving and spilling unexpectedly out onto the road after a fitful rainy night, or pelting you in storms with pebbles (or worse) like mischievous giant children unaccustomed to their own strength. I've driven that winding stretch at night when the roadway looked like the surface of the moon, stones and boulders strewn across it in ghostly moonshadows, and not a car in sight in either direction for a hundred miles. When that happens, you have to weave and pick your way among rocks large enough to crater a tire or an oilpan, now and then stopping and getting out to move a few stones to make a path. Residents in these parts tend to carry a sleeping bag in the trunk in winter, because you never know when you might get caught overnight between slides. That's never happened to me in all these years; but if it did, it could be a long cold night waiting for Caltrans to show up and clear the road at dawn.

Nobody knows exactly when the first humans poured down the California coast from the Bering Land Bridge, sometime in the last days of the last Ice Age. It had to have been after the glaciers had begun receding from the shoreline, but before there had been enough melting to drown those first settlements under hundreds of feet of seawater. There's no chance of finding their remains today. We do know that shell and bone middens on the Esalen property itself date back as much as six thousand years, tidy relics of the Esselen Indians, or their predecessors who roamed these hills and camped by these healing springs for many millennia before being decimated, mostly by the diseases brought by the Europeans, the microbes racing raced ahead of the advancing Spaniards just a couple of centuries ago. Ranchers took over the South Coast of Big Sur after that. It was remote, outlaw territory down to the 1930s, when Roosevelt's New Deal brought the highway through at last, putting the region within an hour or so from town instead of a day, bringing Big Sur more or less into the twentieth century.

It was this magic shelf of cliffs and springs, 27 acres of gardens and stream between highway and beach, that drew Michael Murphy and Richard Price at the beginning of the '60s, two young dreamers short on cash but long on chutzpah, to found what soon became, and still is, the Esalen Institute. Both were grad school dropouts (Mike from philosophy at Stanford, Dick from psychology at Harvard—an uneasy trade-off that long characterized the institute they founded); both were mistrustful of the kind of education they'd left behind them, and both were determined to create something radically different from the august institutions they'd rejected—and been rejected by.

Their dream: to found, in Mike's words, "an experimental venue, a forum for everything excluded from 'the Academy' of the day"—by which they meant the mainstream universities and research institutes of those post-war, Eisenhower, gray-flannel times. The project sounded quixotic, but it had the blessing of no less a visionary than Aldous Huxley, who was soon to become one of the first presenters showcased at Esalen. Some further assets: Dick's family had some money, which he might or might not be able to draw on. Most importantly, Mike's grandmother was looking for something to do with her Big Sur Hot Springs Creek property, a dramatic but not very lucrative relic of her doctor husband's 1910 scheme of opening a Victorian hot-baths spa. That scheme had foundered on the impossibility of good road access; then came World War I, and Victorian spa-cures went out of fashion. The senior Murphys had since built a summer home on one side of the creek, and there was a small motel-cum-baths concession known as Slate's Hot Springs on the other, much in need of new management at the time. (This management disarray may have been exemplified by the fact that the caretaker/gatekeeper at the time was none other than Hunter S. Thompson, not yet legendary as the creator of gonzo journalism of the '60s and '70s. Locally, he was already legendary for combining morning drinking with target practice up at the highway gate).

Such were their early project resources, especially the property and the chutzpah. What they didn't have was a business model, any clear curriculum, or much of a plan for what would happen in the "seminars" they envisioned. Basically their approach involved making up invitation lists of everybody they'd ever wanted to meet, visionaries and innovators who'd been excluded or extruded from academia, or had simply outgrown it: names like Bucky Fuller, Alan Watts, Timothy Leary, Richard Alpert, Huxley himself—all soon to be joined of course by Fritz Perls, Stan Grof, Gregory Bateson, Erik Erickson, and literally hundreds more, famous and not, outrageous and otherwise, and on down to the parallel figures today (Rupert Sheldrake, Dan Siegel, Jon Kabat-Zinn, and scores more like them).

"And to our amazement," (still the words of founder Murphy) "they all came!" And with them came the students, by the hundreds. Once there, of course they had to figure out what to do with them, since traditional classroom lectures in rows were certainly not what anybody had come for. And so "workshop education" was born.

And the rest, as they say, is history. You can read all about it in Jeffrey Kripal's handsome, readable tome *Esalen: America and the Religion of No Religion*—"all" being sex and drugs and Beatles and Baez in the old days—and Cold War diplomacy, the transformation of education, health, spiritual practices, consciousness research, psychology and psychotherapy and the new field of lifelong "personal growth," economic and ecologic studies, ESP and remote prayer effects, and much, much more.

By any measure, Murphy and Price's "experiment" has been a wild (at times, literally wild) success. Nor has that just been a matter of the celebrity teachers, the solid lineup of courses and the scores of books over the years, or the literally thousands who will tell you their lives were changed at Esalen. To take the measure of the experiment, think of the list of areas taken up for study, research, pro bono conferencing, platforming, midwifing, or other forms of nurture and promotion at Esalen over the decades: areas like lifelong education (whoever heard of that in the 1950s?); "personal growth" itself (ditto); "track two" and "citizen diplomacy" in the face of two hostile Cold-War governments (Murphy, the Irish-American, likes to brag that he is the only person in history known to have been subject to recruitment attempts by the CIA, the KGB, and Sinn Féin!—unsuccessfully in all cases, he hastens to add); integral health and complementary medicine (unknown terms a generation ago); somatic studies (ditto); mind-body studies and practices (ditto); the introduction and "westernization" of yoga, meditation, and other Eastern philosophies and practices (Murphy's seminal influence was and remains Sri Aurobindo, the Indian philosopher-saint *and* political radical—a quintessential Esalen combo); experiential education itself; sustainability and ecological education; and the list goes on and on.

Including of course the "human potential," once known as the "human potential movement"—a phrase that was created for the media by Esalen's own George Leonard out of Huxley's "human potentialities." If the phrase sounds quaint and newagey today, that's because the New Age has long since gone mainstream (imagine your world without some of the above-listed resources). Meanwhile, Esalen has moved on to new initiatives, new edges where the known meets the about-to-be-known (like the integration of science and spirituality, or evolutionary theory and consciousness studies). This is the young, restless spirit of Big Sur still at work, still looking out in our sometimes darkening world on the edge of a continent where the West looks out toward the East, still questing for that integral "something" that unites seeming opposites into the alchemy of something new.

Contributors' Notes

Carolyn See has written nine novels and several non-fiction books. She is a professor emerita at UCLA and is Friday Morning Book Reviewer for the Washington Post. She has been a board member of PEN Center USA West, National Book Critics Circle and the Miracle Project, and is a Getty and Guggenheim Fellow.

Charles Hood has seen over 500 different species of wild bird in California and its waters, and has been to all 58 counties, even the ones nobody remembers. From Red Hen Press, he is the co-author of *Río de Dios: Thirteen Histories of the Los Angeles River*. Current book projects include Antarctica, the wildlife of India, and a survey of the 190 moons of our solar system.

Dana Goodyear is a staff writer at *The New Yorker* and the author of *Honey and Junk*, a collection of poems. She teaches literary nonfiction, with an emphasis on new media, at the University of Southern California, and is a co-founder and co-president of Figment, a youth-oriented mobile platform for reading and writing fiction.

Pam Waterman is a garden writer/lecturer/photographer/garden tour leader who has published articles in *The Los Angeles Times, Beautiful Gardens, Pacific Horticulture, Southern California Gardener, Boy's Life, Lifescapes* and *Flower and Garden*. She lives in Pasadena and writes a garden column for the San Gabriel Valley newspaper group that includes the *Pasadena Star News*.

An avid traveler, she has visited, photographed, and lectured on gardens in the United States, China, Japan, Vietnam, South Africa, South America, New Zealand, Australia, and most European countries.

She tends a hillside garden shaded by two venerable pine trees and cares for more than 400 potted plants. She often dreams of having a sunny garden.

Terry Wolverton is author of seven books: *Embers*, a novel-in-poems; *Insurgent Muse: life and art at the Woman's Building*, a memoir; *The Labrys Reunion* and *Bailey's Beads*, novels; and three collections of poetry: *Black Slip*, *Mystery Bruise* and *Shadow and Praise*. A new novel, *Stealing Angel*, will be published in 2011. She has also edited fourteen literary anthologies, including *Mischief, Caprice, and Other Poetic Strategies*. She is the founder of Writers At Work, a creative writing center in Los Angeles, where she teaches fiction, creative nonfiction, and poetry.

Celeste Fremon is an award winning freelance journalist and the author of *G-Dog and the Homeboys* and the upcoming, *An American Family*. She is the creator and editor of WitnessLA.com, a Senior Fellow for Social Justice/New Media at the Institute for Justice and Journalism, an adjunct professor at the USC Annenberg School of Journalism, and a Visiting Lecturer at UC Irvine where she teaches literary journalism as it relates to social justice.

David L. Ulin is book editor of the *Los Angeles Times*. He is the author of *The Myth of Solid Ground: Earthquakes, Prediction, and the Fault Line Between Reason and Faith*, and the editor of *Another City: Writing From Los Angeles*, and *Writing Los Angeles; A Literary Anthology*, which won a 2002 California Book Award. His new book, *The Lost Art of Reading*, will be published in the fall.

Scott Timberg was born in Palo Alto and moved to Los Angeles from the East Coast in his late twenties after realizing the error of his ways. He's been a staff arts writer at *New Times LA* and the *Los Angeles Times*. With Dana Gioia, he co-edited *The Misread City: New Literary Los Angeles*, for Red Hen Press. He is currently a freelance writer on music, film and books and his work has appeared in *The New York Times* and *GQ*. He runs the blog *The Misread City: West Coast Culture and Beyond* and lives in the foothills outside the city with his wife and son.

Benjamin Schwarz is the national and literary editor of *The Atlantic*.

Christina Schwarz's novels include *Drowning Ruth* and *All Is Vanity*.

Denise Hamilton writes the *Eve Diamond* series and is editor of *Los Angeles Noir*, an anthology of new writing that spent two months on bestseller lists, won the Edgar Award for Best Short Story and the Southern California Independent Booksellers' award for Best Mystery of the Year. *Los Angeles Noir 2: The Classics*, will be published in April 2010. Denise's most recent novel, *The Last Embrace*, was a Los Angeles Times bestseller set in 1949 Hollywood and has been compared to James Ellroy and Raymond Chandler. Denise's books have been shortlisted for the Edgar, Macavity, Anthony and Willa Cather awards. Her debut *The Jasmine Trade* was a finalist for the prestigious Creasey Dagger Award given by the UK Crime Writers Association. Hamilton's books have been BookSense 76 picks, USA Today Summer Picks and Best Books of the Year by the *Los Angeles Times*, the *South Florida Sun-Sentinel* and the *Toronto Globe & Mail*. Prior to writing novels, Hamilton was a *Los Angeles Times* staff writer. Her award-winning stories have also appeared in *Wired, Cosmopolitan, Der Spiegel* and *New Times*. She covered the collapse of Communism and was a Fulbright Scholar in Yugoslavia during the Bosnian War. Hamilton lives in the Los Angeles suburbs with her husband and two boys.

Jenny Price is a writer, Los Angeles Urban Ranger, and Research Scholar at the UCLA Center for the Study of Women. Author of "Thirteen Ways of Seeing Nature in L.A." and *Flight Maps: Adventures with Nature in Modern America*, she's written also for *GOOD, Sunset, Believer, Audubon, New York Times,* and *Los Angeles Times,* and writes the "Green Me Up, JJ" column on *LA Observed*. She gives frequent tours of the L.A. River, has a Ph.D. in history from Yale University, and is currently living on Venice Beach.

D.J. Waldie is the author of *Holy Land: A Suburban Memoir* and other books. He is a contributing editor for the *Los Angeles Times* and a contributing writer for *Los Angeles* magazine. He is the deputy city manager of Lakewood, California.

Deanne Stillman is a widely published, critically acclaimed writer. Her books include *Mustang: The Saga of the Wild Horse in the American West*, a *Los Angeles Times* Best Book 2008 and winner of the California Book Award silver medal for nonfiction; and *Twentynine Palms: A True Story of Murder, Marines, and the Mojave*, a cult classic which Hunter Thompson called "a strange and brilliant story by an important American writer."

Thomas Curwen is a writer and editor for the Los Angeles Times. His 2007 story "Attacked by a Grizzly" was a finalist for a 2008 Pulitzer Prize in Feature Writing. He edited the *Times' Outdoors* section and from 1996 to 2002 was the deputy editor of the paper's Book Review. His writing has been honored by the American Association of Sunday and Features Editors and the Academy of American Poets.

After graduating from the University of San Francisco in 1962, **Kevin Starr** served two years as a lieutenant in a tank battalion in Germany. He took his MA from Harvard in 1965 and his PhD in 1969. He also holds the degree Master of Library Science from UC Berkeley. Kevin Starr has served as Allston Burr Senior Tutor in Eliot House at Harvard, City Librarian of San Francisco, State Librarian for California, and is currently University Professor and Professor of History at the University of Southern California. His many articles and books, including his *Americans and the California Dream* series, have won him a Guggenheim Fellowship, five honorary doctorates, the Gold and Silver Medals of the Commonwealth Club, membership in the Society of American Historians, the Presidential Medallion from USC, the Centennial Medal from the Graduate School of Arts and Sciences at Harvard, and the Humanities Medal from the National Endowment of the Humanities. Oxford University Press has recently published *Golden Dreams: California in an Age of Abundance, 1950-1963*, and Bloomsbury Press will release in July *Golden Gate Bridge: The Life and Times of America's Greatest Bridge.*

Meghan Daum has written a weekly opinion column for the *Los Angeles Times* since 2005. She is the author of the memoir *Life Would Be Perfect If I Lived In That House* as well as the novel *The Quality of Life Report* and the essay collection *My Misspent Youth*. She lives in Los Angeles.

Erika Schickel is the author of *You're Not the Boss of Me: Adventures of a Modern Mom*. She reviews books and is an op-ed contributor for the *Los Angeles Times*, *The Huffington Post* and *LA Observed*.

Lisa See is the author of the best-selling novels *Snow Flower and the Secret Fan*, *Shanghai Girls*, and *Peony In Love*, as well as the non-fiction family history *On Gold Mountain*. See, the daughter of novelist Carolyn See, is one-eighth Chinese and grew up in Los Angeles surrounded by her Chinese-American family.

T. Jefferson Parker, a native of Los Angeles, began his writing career in 1978 as a reporter for a local weekly newspaper. In 1985 his first novel, *Laguna Heat*, became a best-seller and was made into a film. Since that auspicious beginning, Parker has made a name for himself with a string of award-winning novels that deal with crime, life, and death in sunny Southern California.

Carolyn Kellogg, a regular contributor to the *Los Angeles Times*, earned her MFA in Fiction from the University of Pittsburgh. Her work has appeared in *Bookforum*, *The Morning News*, *Skateboarding Magazine* and *Black Clock*, and she can be heard on NPR. She is at work on a historical fiction—or fictional history—of a family in Los Angeles in the 1920s.

Tony Platt, retired from university teaching at Sacramento State University, is a writer and secretary of the Coalition to Protect Yurok Cultural Legacies at O-pyúweg (Big Lagoon). He is writing a book on this topic, *Grave Matters*, for Heyday. His posts about his current research are at http://goodtogo.typepad.com.

Mark Arax, who lives and writes amid the raisin fields of Fresno, is the author of *West of the West*, *In My Father's Name* and the co-author of *The King of California*.

Louise Steinman is the author of two books, most recently *The Souvenir: A Daughter Discovers Her Father's War* ("…an intimate and powerful story of the effects of war.") Her first book, *The Knowing Body: The Artist as Storyteller in Contemporary Performance* was hailed by the L.A. Times as a "dazzling study of the performing arts." She is currently completing *The Crooked Mirror: A Conversation with Poland*, about Jewish-Polish reconciliation.

Since 1993, she has curated the award-winning ALOUD literary series for the Library Foundation of Los Angeles. She is also co-director of the Los Angeles Institute for Humanities, USC.

James Brown is the author of several novels, and the memoirs *The Los Angeles Diaries* and *This River*. His creative non-fiction has appeared in *GQ*, *The New York Times Magazine*, *The Los Angeles Times Magazine*, *Esquire* and *Ploughshares*. He is the recipient of a National Endowment for the Arts Fellowship in Creative Writing and the Nelson Algren Award in Short Fiction. Brown teaches in the M.F.A. Program at Cal State San Bernardino, and lives in Lake Arrowhead, California, with his wife and writer Paula Priamos-Brown.

Susan Straight has published six novels, including *A Million Nightingales* (2006, Anchor Books) and *Highwire Moon* (2001, Anchor Books). Her new novel, *Take One Candle Light a Room*, will be published in October 2010 by Pantheon. She has published stories and essays in many magazines, including *Harpers*, *The New York Times*, *The Los Angeles Times*, *Salon*, and *Zoetrope All-Story*. She was born in Riverside, where she lives with her three daughters.

Jenny Factor serves on the Core Faculty of Antioch University Los Angeles' low-residency MFA in Creative Writing program—the nation's only MFA devoted to literature and the pursuit of social justice. Her poetry collection, *Unraveling at the Name* (Copper Canyon Press) received a Hayden Carruth Award and was a finalist in for a Lambda Literary Award. After graduating from Harvard College and the Bennington Writing Seminars, Jenny worked as an editor, a contract archaeologist, and a Montessori preschool teacher. She lives in the San Gabriel Valley with her partner and son.

David Kipen is the author of *The Schreiber Theory: A Radical Rewrite of American Film History*, and translator of Cervantes' *The Dialogue of the Dogs*. Until January 2010, Kipen was the literature director of the National Endowment of the Arts, where he directed the Big Read and the Guadalajara Book Festival initiatives. He also served from 1998 to 2005 as book critic, and before that book editor, for the *San Francisco Chronicle*. California state librarian and historian Kevin Starr has said of him, "I can personally testify to Mr. Kipen's scholarship, probity, socialization, and good humor," which Kipen still hasn't gotten over.

David St. John has been honored, over the course of his career, with many of the most significant prizes for poets, including both the Prix de Rome Fellowship and an Award in Literature from the American Academy and Institute of Arts and Letters, and the O. B. Hardison Prize (a career award for teaching and poetic achievement) from The Folger Shakespeare Library. He is the author of nine collections of poetry (including *Study for the World's Body*, nominated for The National Book Award in Poetry), most recently *The Face: A Novella in Verse*. He is also the co-editor, with

Cole Swensen, of *American Hybrid: A Norton Anthology of New Poetry*. David St. John lives in Venice Beach.

Rob Roberge is the author of the story collection *Working Backwards from the Worst Moment of My Life* (Red Hen, Oct. 2010) and the novels, *More Than They Could Chew* (Dark Alley/Harper Collins, 2005) and *Drive* (Hollyridge Press reissue, 2006). Stories have been featured in *ZYZZYVA*, *Chelsea*, *Other Voices*, *Alaska Quarterly Review*, and the "Ten Writers Worth Knowing Issue" of *The Literary Review*. His work has also been anthologized in *Another City* (City Lights, 2001), *It's All Good* (Manic D Press, 2004) and *SANTI: Lives of the Modern Saints* (Black Arrow Press, 2007).

Rob also plays guitar and sings with the LA area garage bands, The Violet Rays, The Danbury Shakes and veteran LA avant-punk pioneers, The Urinals.

For more info: www.robroberge.com.

Lillian Vallee is an award-winning translator, writer and scholar who served an apprenticeship with Polish poet Czeslaw Milosz. Her poems appear in *Highway 99, A Literary Journey through California's Great Central Valley*; *Two-hearted Oak*; *Collision*, and in three chapbooks—*Vision at Orestimba*, *Erratics*, and *handful of snow*. She writes a popular monthly column ("Rivers of Birds, Forests of Tules: Central Valley Nature and Culture in Season") documenting her bioregional passions.

Tim Z. Hernandez is an award winning writer and performer from California's San Joaquin Valley. His work has been published in numerous anthologies and his performances featured across the U.S. His debut book of poetry, *Skin Tax*, received the 2006 American Book Award, and the James Duval Phelan Award from the San Francisco Foundation. His debut novel, *Breathing, In Dust* was published in early 2010 to critical acclaim. He received his B.A. in Writing & Literature from Naropa University and attends the Writing Seminars at Bennington College in Vermont. He lives in Fresno, California with his wife and children, where he works to restore the San Joaquin River.

Janet Fitch is the author of the novels *Paint It Black*, published in 2006, and *White Oleander*, an Oprah book club selection which appeared in 1999, and was made into a feature film in 2002. Fitch's short stories have appeared in such anthologies and journals as *Black Clock*, *Room of One's Own*, *Speakeasy*, *Black Warrior Review*, *Rain City Review*, and *Los Angeles Noir*. She currently teaches creative writing in the MPW program at the University of Southern California and the Squaw Valley Community of Writers summer workshops. She lives in Los Angeles.

Seth Greenland is the author of the novels *Shining City* and *The Bones*. His produced plays include *Jungle Rot* (winner Kennedy Center/American Express Fund for New American Plays Award and American Theatre Critics Association Award), *Jerusalem* and *Red Memories*. He lives in Los Angeles.

Andrew Lam is a writer and an editor with the Pacific News Service, and a short story writer. He co-founded New America Media, an association of over 2000 ethnic media organizations in America. He also contributed over sixty commentaries to NPR's *All Things Considered* over the last decade. His essays have appeared in dozens of newspapers and magazines across the country. His short stories are also anthologized widely and taught in many universities and colleges, and have appeared in many literary journals. His book, *Perfume Dreams: Reflections on the Vietnamese Diaspora* has won the Pen American Beyond the Margins Award in 2006, and was short-listed for the Asian American Literature Award. His next book, *East Eats West: Writing in Two Hemispheres* will be published in September 2010. He has just finished a collection of short stories called *Birds of Paradise* and is working on a novel.

Aimee Phan's first book, *We Should Never Meet: Stories* (St. Martin's Press, 2004) has won the Association for Asian American Studies Book Award in Prose. It was also named a Notable Book by the Kiriyama Prize in fiction, as well as a finalist for the 2005 Asian American Literary Awards. Her fiction has appeared in *Colorado Review*, *Michigan Quarterly Review*, *Virginia Quarterly Review*, *Chelsea*, *Prairie Schooner* and *Meridian*. Her nonfiction has appeared in the *New York Times*, *USA Today* and the *Oregonian*. She has received a 2010 NEA Fellowship, a Maytag Fellowship from the Iowa Writers' Workshop and a MacDowell Colony Residency.

Matt Shears is the author of the poetry collection, *where a road had been* (BlazeVox 2010). He is the recipient of a Schaeffer Fellowship from the University of Nevada-Las Vegas and received an MFA from the University of Iowa Writers Workshop. His poetry has appeared in *Colorado Review*, *Denver Quarterly*, *Volt*, *Interim* and *Boston Review*, among others. Born and raised in Ohio, he currently resides with his family in Oakland, California.

Kate Gale is Red Hen Press's Managing Editor. She has a BA/MA in English with emphasis on Creative Writing and a Ph.D. in American Literature from Claremont Graduate University. She is a poet and writer with four books of poetry, a novel, a bilingual children's book, editor of three literary anthologies, and has completed the libretto for the opera *Rio de Sangre* by Don Davis, which will soon receive its world premiere.

Patt Morrison is a longtime columnist and writer for the *Los Angeles Times*, where she has been part of two Pulitzer Prize-winning teams. She's covered stories as disparate as the space shuttle, the Olympics, the O.J. Simpson case and the death of the Princess of Wales.

As founding host of *Life & Times* on KCET-TV and as a commentator on its successor, *SoCal Connected*, she has won six Emmys and several Golden Mike awards. Her work as host of the daily "Patt Morrison" program on Southern California Public Radio's KPCC, the NPR news affiliate, has also won Golden Mike awards for best public affairs program, along with other honors.

Her award-winning book *Rio LA, Tales from the Los Angeles River* was a bestseller, and her contribution to the Akashic Press mystery short story collection, Los Angeles Noir, won particular praise from critics.

Gordon Wheeler, PhD, is President of the Esalen Institute in Big Sur, California, which each year offers some 15,000 students more than 600 residential programs in how to move through personal growth and healing into transformational service in the world. As a psychologist, Wheeler is known for his work with relational dynamics, couples, intimacy and shame issues, lifelong personal development, and relationship as a spiritual practice. The author of over a dozen books and more than a hundred articles in the field, he teaches and trains other psychologists widely around the world; his work has also been translated into some 20 different languages. Gordon and his wife, Nancy Lunney-Wheeler make their home in Big Sur and Santa Cruz, California.

Veronique De Turenne is a Los Angeles-based journalist, essayist, & playwright. Her literary criticism appears on NPR and in major American newspapers, frequently the *Los Angeles Times*. She is at work on a novel.